surreal meals

cinematic suppers

pot luck dinner parties

enlightening morsels

With love and admiration for aynsley vogel,
debbie jow, and the french fries with aioli at the
waazubee

A Ballantine Book
Published by The Ballantine Publishing Group

www.randomhouse.com/BB/

Library of Congress Cataloging-in-Publication Data
Blumer, Bob.
Off the eaten path: inspired recipes for adventurous cooks/recipes,
illustrations, and objets d'art by Bob Blumer.
p. cm.
ISBN 0-345-42150-7 (hc.)
1. Cookery. I. Title.

TX714 .B63 2000
641.5 21—da21
                                        99-012488

Book design by Rodney Bowes

Cover image by Andreas Fitzner, Vienna Paint

Manufactured in the United States of America

First Edition: May 2000

10 9 8 7 6 5 4 3 2 1

introduction

Eight years ago I lost my mind and found my calling. In the ensuing quest to become the patron saint of dysfunctional kitchens, short attention spans, and mismatched place settings, I put my day job on hold, unplugged the phone, and locked myself up with a PowerBook and some art supplies. As the sparks flew, I committed my entire cooking repertoire to paper. When I emerged two months later, I had channeled a cookbook. Well, it wasn't exactly a cookbook. It was a guide to better living that combined my passion for cooking and illustrating with my knack for living beyond my means. I still don't know if it was due to naïveté, tenacity, or good karma, but I managed to talk my way into a publisher's office and walk out with a modest publishing deal. After the book's release, I was unceremoniously thrust onto the talk-show circuit. To compensate for my lack of culinary confidence, I incorporated an element of performance art into each of my appearances. That was the beginning of my odyssey off the eaten path. Six years, seven sauté pans, three hundred thousand air miles, and one book later, the madness finally overthrew my life and became my accidental career.

Along the way I have met and befriended some of the country's most respected chefs and winemakers. Through practice and osmosis, my cooking skills have caught up with my enthusiasm, and the mysteries of wine have begun to unmask themselves. Together they have spawned opportunities I could never have imagined. One day I am preparing a Surreal dinner at the Salvador Dali Museum or designing a faux-supermodel diet for RuPaul, and a week later I am running the celebrated Medoc Marathon in Bordeaux, where the pit stops are stocked with grand cru wines and fresh Atlantic oysters.

Variety is the spice of life, but my favorite role is providing the spark that ignites the culinary creativity hidden in everyone. I take great pleasure in demonstrating how cooking can become the springboard to a higher quality of life—whether you are making an intimate dinner for two, entertaining friends, or ironing a midnight snack.

The epicenter of my recipe-testing and dinner party "research" is my Pee-wee's Playhouse–like kitchen, in which the eccentric collectibles far outnumber the functional appliances. This low-tech playground is anchored by an ancient butcher block, a George Jetson refrigerator, and a forty-year-old gas stove with a mind of its own. The cupboards are practically bare of canned goods, but the counters overflow with seasonal produce, and a selection of quality oils and spices are always within arm's reach.

The recipes in this book have come from many sources. Some I've invented, some I've interpreted, and a few I've coaxed. To make the cut, each recipe must fulfill the arbitrary but uncompromising Surreal Gourmet standards: it must rely on common ingredients brought to life with a heavy-handed infusion of fresh herbs and spices; it must require little in the way of technology or expertise and be very forgiving; its fresh ingredients and creative presentation should do most of the hard work; and the recipe should be simple enough to be incorporated into any cooking repertoire but memorable enough to become addictive.

After eight years on the foodie circuit, I still love shopping for each meal, then bringing home the groceries and blowing up the kitchen. Sure, I still burn stuff and set off the smoke alarm, but that only adds to the spectacle my friends have come to expect. You too can throw together impressive meals with minimal appliances and a few fresh ingredients. Add an unconventional cooking method, a clever theme, or an artistic spin, and you are well on your way off the eaten path.

you are here

This book is divided into six independent sections. Each section diverges into a world of distinctive dining adventures that range from fine art to mad science. Choose any on-ramp, fasten your seat belt, and turn on the gas.

winner dinners Five deceptively simple dinner menus that will transform you into a culinary hero.

extreme cuisine Recipes and detailed instructions for cooking in your dishwasher, on your car engine, with your iron, and in a brown paper lunch bag.

surreal meals Cocktail appetizers and meals concocted from one set of ingredients—but presented to look like something completely different.

cinematic suppers Cocktails, spiced popcorn, and main courses inspired by my five favorite food-related movies—to be enjoyed while watching the video.

pot luck dinner parties Just like a pot luck dinner—but with better odds! Seven friends bring designated ingredients (and a bottle of wine), and you assemble the meal.

enlightening morsels Tips to help make your kitchen more efficient, a crash course on wine that should be easy to swallow, and guerrilla shopping tactics.

signs to look for

To help you enjoy the culinary journey and enhance the overall dining experience, each recipe may be followed by one or more of these signposts:

suggested running order At the end of each Winner Dinner, I have suggested running orders for the advance prep work and the steps to be completed after the guests have arrived. To further help yourself stay focused as the simmering pots and jabbering guests compete for your attention, scribble down this game plan ahead of time and post it by the oven.

le secret There is usually one crucial step or component that can make or break a recipe. If I was at your house while you were cooking one of my dishes, I would uncontrollably gravitate to the kitchen, hover behind you, and point out this important step. Le Secret is my way of doing so in absentia.

the adventure club This is a forum for presenting extra ingredients or twists to take the recipe one step beyond. If you have the time, energy, or interest, take the leap. Otherwise, rest assured that the original recipe is already complete without these additions.

music to cook by/music to dine by/music to wash by Before reinventing myself as The Surreal Gourmet, I worked in the music business managing artists and packaging a variety of recording projects. During that time I was surrounded by music and musicians—many of whom crashed on my couch in their pre-multiplatinum days. Music is still an integral part of my life, and I can't imagine cooking—or eating—without it. My suggestions for Music to Cook By are intended to vibe up your kitchen and stimulate your aural senses. Don't hesitate to *turnip* the volume and sing out of *tuna* (sorry). Music to Dine By has been selected to add a sonic dimension to the meal without drowning out all that stimulating conversation. And Music to Wash By has been chosen to entertain you as you wade through the debris.

recommended wine The more wine I taste, the more I appreciate how a well-chosen bottle can enhance the flavors of a dish—and vice versa. With the excellent advice of several friends in the wine business, I have selected wines that complement each of the entrées in this book and explained the logic behind each choice. My hope is that this information will eventually lead you to your own wine adventures. To allow everyone to find a wine that fits within their price range, I have limited my recommendations to regions and varietals instead of picking specific producers and vintages. These guidelines should also help relieve the anxiety of any guest who calls asking what flavor wine to bring. (See pages 122–127 for a snobbery-free introduction to wine.)

specialized cooking apparatus I have made the assumption that your kitchen is equipped with the bare necessities. If a recipe requires a specialty tool, or any little gizmo that is essential, I have listed it. This should keep you from getting halfway through the recipe and realizing that you have loaned your croque monsieur iron to your neighbor. (See page 129 for the holy trinity of kitchen basics listed in Essential Utensils.)

alternate routes

deserted desserts I love to eat dessert, but I always exceed my pain threshold in the kitchen before there is time to make it. When the editor of my first book insisted that I at least address the "issue," I listed my Ten Favorite Ways to Avoid Making Dessert. In my second book, just when they thought they had me cornered, I devised Ten More Ways to Avoid Making Dessert. After twenty suggestions (nineteen if you don't count "have sex instead"), I've pretty well maxed-out on excuses. For this book, I've taken a stab at a few easy-but-impressive desserts. Otherwise you are on your own to wing it, buy it, or delegate it to the first guest who calls offering to bring something—if they didn't mean it, they shouldn't have asked.

eat, drink, and take taxis Since the publication of my last book, I have submerged myself in the world of fine wine and spirits. Now, I am more enthusiastic than ever about enhancing my dinners with bottled poetry. Not everyone is as excitable. Help abstainers feel equally welcome at any occasion by providing a selection of nonalcoholic alternatives such as freshly squeezed juices and freshly brewed coffee. And if any of your guests drink *too* enthusiastically, don't let them drive off until they can name all of the seven seas, seven dwarfs, seven sins, and seven wonders of the world.

winner dinners

Food brings friends together. As our friendships and our palates evolve, so do our dining standards. Sharing the moment in fine dining establishments is always a nice way to go, as long as the maître d' knows who you think you are, and you can borrow the cellular phone from the next table to get your credit limit increased by the time the inattentive waiter brings your check. Cooking at home eliminates these distractions and lets you up the ante. It also affords you the luxury of purchasing the highest-quality ingredients and indulging in wines that would be out of your range at restaurant prices.

Four is a very harmonious number to cook for. Meals can be prepared easily with even the most limited kitchen arsenal; servingware isn't an issue (nobody said anything about it matching); and conversations flow easily and intimately, with no one getting left out in the cold. And with four diners, you can pour out a different bottle of wine with each course, which allows you the opportunity to dabble in the art of food-and-wine pairing. (See pages 123 and 127 for a quick lesson in pairing.)

The format of the following dinners is set up the same way I serve in my home. As the guests arrive, I draw them into my world with the cocktail du jour. (Most people are willing to forgo their "usual" and try any potion once—as long as it sounds enticing.) Then I serve the appetizer and everyone mingles. When the mood seems right, I slide into the kitchen to finish the main course and side dishes. Instead of thinking of this time away from the party as an interruption, I see it as an opportunity to invite one of the guests into my inner sanctum for some one-on-one quality time. When the final prep is done, dinner is served. To minimize the work, dessert is improvised, imported, or ignored.

Each Winner Dinner infuses premium ingredients with bold flavors that are guaranteed to start a party on the collective palate. Individually, each course is a conquest, but together they will transform you into a culinary hero.

nuevo noche mexicano

nuevo mexicano noche

★ frozen watermelon margarita ★ mango & brie quesadilla ★
★ seared ahi tuna taco with avocado salsa ★
★ roasted corn & black bean relish ★ café olé & a donut ★

dinner for 4

For hundreds of years, margaritas meant lime, quesadillas meant Jack cheese, and tacos meant ground beef. Then, in the '80s frenzy of fusion cooking, Wolfgang Puck put smoked salmon on pizza, and the sacred cows of ethnic cuisine were all led to slaughter. Many of the resulting who'd-a-thunk-it combinations, like these, are so good, it's hard to imagine going back to the originals.

suggested running order for advance prep
1 cut, seed, and freeze watermelon 2 make mango quesadilla filling 3 skin and slice Brie 4 prepare quesadilla dipping sauce 5 make avocado salsa 6 roast peppers for corn salsa 7 make dry rub for tuna 8 make corn relish

total advance prep time 1 1/2 hours

suggested running order for cooking once the guests have arrived
1 make cocktail 2 make quesadillas 3 sear tuna and dice 4 heat taco shells
5 assemble tacos and serve with salsa 6 make coffee and assemble dessert

total kitchen duty after guests have arrived 20 minutes

music to cook by Los Super Seven. *Los Super Seven.* Tex-Mex and Chicano artists, featuring members of Los Lobos and Texas Tornadoes, team up for an exploration of their musical heritage.

music to dine by Linda Ronstadt. *Canciones de mi padre.* Authentic Mexicano.

music to wash by El Vez. *Graciasland.* Viva Las Vegas! meets Viva La Raza! The Mexican Elvis dishes up equal portions of humor, social satire, and rock 'n' roll.

recommended wine Mexican beer is the perfect foil for this spicy meal. If you want to stick with wine, choose an "off dry" German Riesling. It is sweet enough to temper the spices of the tuna and delicate enough to underscore the avocado salsa.

frozen watermelon margarita

serves 4

**Even if you're the type who resists change,
I think you'll find this one easy to swallow.**

2¹/2 cups seedless (or seeded)
  watermelon, *cut into 1-inch cubes,
  rind discarded before measuring*
3 tablespoons freshly squeezed lime juice
4 ounces tequila (ideally, an aged tequila)
2 ounces Cointreau or triple sec
1¹/2 cups ice

1 Put cut watermelon in a plastic bag and place
  in freezer for 2 hours. (If time does not permit
  this step, add a few extra ice cubes when
  blending; the difference is not that significant.)
2 Stuff all ingredients into a blender and puree
  until smooth. Garnish with a watermelon
  wedge and serve immediately.

le secret Buy seedless watermelon.
the adventure club Do tequila shooters out of
the hollowed-out lime halves.
tips for advance prep Watermelon can be cut,
seeded, and frozen up to several days in advance.
specialized cooking apparatus blender

mango & brie quesadilla
with sour cream & lime dipping sauce

serves 4

The unconventional alliance of tropical fruit and French cheese will help set the tone for the evening.

4	(8-inch) flour tortillas (available in all grocery stores but sometimes hidden in the refrigerated or frozen-food sections)
2	jalapeño chilies, *seeds and membranes discarded, minced*
2	scallions, *trimmed and chopped finely*
1	ripe mango, *peeled, pitted, and diced* (If unavailable, replace with papaya or pear)
2/3	cup lightly packed fresh cilantro leaves, *chopped, stems discarded before measuring*
8	ounces Brie, *sliced into long 1/4-inch slices* (rind removal is optional—but I always remove it.)

mango & brie quesadilla

1 Heat a 10-inch nonstick sauté pan over medium-high heat. Place 1 tortilla in the dry pan for approximately 1 minute per side, or until it begins to brown. Remove. Repeat with the second tortilla. (If your tortilla expands like a blowfish, poke it with a fork to release the hot air.)

2 After the second tortilla has browned, leave it in the pan and reduce heat to medium-low. Spread half the mango mixture evenly over the tortilla, then top with half the Brie strips. Top with the first tortilla. Cover the pan with a lid and cook for 2 minutes.

3 Flip the quesadilla with a spatula, re-cover the pan, and continue cooking for 2 more minutes. (Don't worry if a bit of cheese escapes and begins to sizzle loudly.)

4 Remove the quesadilla from the pan, let sit for 1 minute, then slice into 8 wedges (like a pizza). Serve immediately with the sour cream dip.

5 Repeat with the remaining ingredients.

sour cream & lime dipping sauce

2	limes
1/4	teaspoon salt
1/4	cup sour cream or plain yogurt

1 Zest 1 lime (see page 140), then juice it. Blend the zest, 1 1/2 tablespoons lime juice, salt, and sour cream with a fork until the mixture is smooth. Transfer to a small decorative bowl or teacup and refrigerate.

2 In a small bowl, combine 1 tablespoon lime juice, mango, jalapeños, scallions, and cilantro. Mix thoroughly with a fork. Set aside.

le secret Use a very ripe mango (ripe = fragrant and yields slightly to the firm touch).
tips for advance prep Mango mixture and dipping sauce may be prepared up to a day in advance and refrigerated.
specialized cooking apparatus nonstick pan with lid; zester or fine grater

seared ahi tuna taco with avocado salsa

serves 4

The proliferation of Mexican fast food has made the taco as common as the cheeseburger. With the help of a searing tutorial from one of my favorite hot tamales, Mary Sue Milliken, I have elevated the taco to gourmet status.

seared ahi tuna taco

1	teaspoon ground cumin
$1/4$	teaspoon cayenne pepper
$1/2$	teaspoon salt
$1/2$	tablespoon freshly ground black pepper
$1/2$	teaspoon ground coriander
12	ounces ahi (or albacore) tuna, *cut into 1-inch-thick steaks*
$1/2$	tablespoon olive oil
8	taco shells (available in most grocery stores)
2	limes, *halved*

1 In a small bowl, combine cumin, cayenne, salt, pepper, and coriander.
2 Rub spice mixture generously on both sides of the tuna.
3 Preheat oven to 350°F for the taco shells.
4 Heat a nonstick pan over high heat. When pan is smoking hot, add olive oil, wait 10 seconds, then add tuna. Sear for 1 minute per side, or until fish is cooked on the outside, but rare on the inside. Transfer to a plate.
5 Separate taco shells and place them in the oven for 4 minutes (timing is everything here, since they go from perfectly done to burned after about 1 additional minute).
6 While the shells are heating, dice tuna into $1/4$-inch cubes.

To serve, fill taco shells halfway with salsa. Spoon tuna over salsa and squeeze a spritz of lime juice overtop. Serve immediately.

avocado salsa

2	ripe (but not too mushy) avocados, *pit and skin discarded, diced into $1/4$-inch cubes*
2	medium tomatoes, *diced into $1/4$-inch cubes*
1	cup lightly packed fresh cilantro leaves, *minced, stems discarded before measuring*
$1/4$	cup red onion, *diced*
3	tablespoons freshly squeezed lemon juice
$1/8$	teaspoon salt
$1/8$	teaspoon freshly ground black pepper

1 Add all ingredients to a medium-size bowl. Toss gently. DO NOT mash avocado.

le secret Do not overcook tuna.
tips for advance prep The dry rub can be made ahead and stored in a sealed jar. It lasts almost indefinitely.

roasted corn & black bean relish

serves 4

This side dish is the perfect compadre for any Mexican or Tex-Mex meal.

1	poblano chili, or 2 jalepeño chilies
1	red bell pepper
4	ears corn, *husked*, or 1^1/2 cups frozen corn kernels
2	tablespoons butter
1	cup canned black beans, *drained and rinsed*
1	cup lightly packed cilantro leaves, *chopped finely, stems discarded before measuring*
3	scallions, *trimmed and chopped finely*
1	tablespoon olive oil
1	tablespoon balsamic vinegar
1	tablespoon freshly squeezed lime juice
^{1}/2	teaspoon salt
^{1}/2	teaspoon freshly ground black pepper

1 Roast poblano and bell peppers directly on a gas or electric stove element. Rotate ^{1}/4 turn as the skin blackens. This should take about 2 minutes per side. When the peppers are fully blackened, seal them in a paper bag for 5 minutes, then peel off and discard their blackened skins. Discard seeds and membranes, and dice peppers finely.

2 Using a sharp knife, separate the corn kernels from the cob (see diagram). *If you are using frozen corn, go directly to step 3.*

3 Melt butter in a sauté pan over medium-high heat. Add corn and sauté for 8 minutes, until the kernels begin to show a hint of brown.

4 In a large bowl, combine corn, beans, peppers, cilantro, and scallions. Add oil, vinegar, lime juice, salt, and black pepper. Toss thoroughly.

le secret Off-season "fresh" corn is often tough and tasteless. Unless the kernels look plump and inviting, use frozen corn.

the adventure club Roast corn in its husk over a wood grill for 12 minutes, or until the husks char and the kernels begin to caramelize (in this case, decob kernels after cob has cooled and skip step 3).

tips for advance prep Relish may be made up to a day in advance and refrigerated. Allow to warm to room temperature before serving.

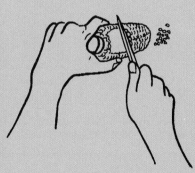

café olé & a donut

serves 4

Churros, commonly sold by Mexican street vendors, are deep-fried dough treats rolled in cinnamon sugar. If you live near a Latino grocery, you might be lucky enough to find them. Otherwise, cinnamon donuts are all it takes to indulge your guests' dunking desires.

4	cups strongly brewed coffee (see page 50)
1	ounce bittersweet chocolate
4	ounces Kahlúa
8	tablespoons whipped cream (real or aerosol)
4	cinnamon donuts (Hostess crumb are my favorite.)

1 Pour coffee into four preheated cups. Don't fill to top.
2 Add $1/4$ ounce of chocolate and 1 ounce of Kahlúa to each cup. Let sit for 1 minute, then stir. Top with whipped cream. Encourage guests to dunk their donuts in coffee.

the even easier way out Serve chocolate-covered espresso beans.

slammin' salmon extravaganza

slammin' salmon extravaganza

★ raspberry martini ★ gee, your beet smells terrific ★
★ pepper-crusted maple-glazed salmon ★
★ (i can't believe it's not) creamed corn ★
★ grilled raisin bread, stilton & pear dessertwich ★

dinner for 4

This meal is an exquisite example of the whole being greater than the sum of its parts.
But don't be fooled by the simplicity of the recipes—simplicity is the secret to their success.

suggested running order for advance prep
1 marinate salmon (ideally the day before) **2** bake beets **3** prepare corn **4** prepare pears **5** prepare beets and endives and assemble beet bites

total advance prep time 2 hours, with time off while the beets bake (Note: This does not include marinating time for salmon.)

suggested running order for cooking once the guests have arrived
1 preheat oven **2** make cocktail and serve beets **3** crust salmon with pepper and bake **4** heat corn **5** assemble plates and serve **6** make dessert

total kitchen duty after guests have arrived 25 minutes
music to cook by Henry Mancini. *The Pink Panther Strikes Again.* Does your feeesh bite?

music to dine by Morcheeba. *Who Can You Trust?* This hypnotic album is the perfect combination of melodic hooks and ambient grooves.

music to wash by Ashley McIssac. *Hi, How Are You Today?* This young Cape Breton fiddle player colors his traditional fiddling with a bad-assed rock 'n' roll attitude. An awesome, albeit hard-to-find, disc.

recommended wine A young Alsace Riesling. This is a fruity wine with little residual sugar, which plays well off the maple sweetness of the salmon.

raspberry martini

serves 4

This cocktail tastes like raspberry nectar, but it is 100 percent alcohol. Do not allow your guests to drive, operate heavy machinery, or tango after consuming more than two.

5	ounces vodka
1 1/2	ounces Chambord or framboise (raspberry liqueur)
1 1/2	ounces Cointreau or triple sec
2	cups ice

1 Fill a martini shaker or a large glass with ice. Add ingredients and shake or stir. Strain into four chilled martini glasses. Garnish with a fresh raspberry or an orange twist.

2 Repeat if necessary.

gee, your beet smells terrific

serves 4

Roasting beets concentrates their natural sugars and fills the kitchen with an intoxicating aroma. This cooking method transforms them from a misunderstood vegetable into a candylike treat. The additional ingredients in this reconfigured beet salad recipe play off the natural sweetness to create a bite-size appetizer that will seduce beet lovers and instantly alter the consciousness of beet-phobics.

3	medium-size beets, *tops discarded*
2	teaspoons olive oil
1	teaspoon balsamic vinegar
1	teaspoon freshly squeezed orange juice
2	teaspoons fresh tarragon (optional), *stems discarded before measuring, chopped finely*
1/4	teaspoon freshly ground black pepper
1	ounce strong goat cheese, *diced into 1/8-inch cubes*
3	tablespoons toasted hazelnuts or walnuts (see page 133)
2	Belgian endives, *separated and washed* (If you can't find endives, replace with the very inside section of a head of romaine lettuce or good old reliable Ritz crackers.)

1 Bake whole, unskinned beets for $1^1/2$ to 2 hours at 400°F (longer if they are more than 3 inches in diameter). Place a sheet of aluminum foil on the rack below to catch the natural juice drippings.
2 Remove from oven and allow to cool.
3 Peel and discard skin. Then slice and dice beets finely.
4 Combine oil, vinegar, orange juice, pepper, and tarragon in a bowl. Add beets, cheese, and nuts. Toss gently.

To serve, spoon a tablespoon of beet salad onto the bottom end of individual endive leaves.

le secret Don't be put off by the blackened exterior of the baking beets. The longer the beets bake, the sweeter they become.
the adventure club Use golden beets and/or replace olive oil with hazelnut or walnut oil.
tips for advanced prep Beets can be baked and refrigerated in their skin up to 2 days in advance. The beet mixture can be assembled several hours in advance, but don't spoon the mixture onto the endive leaves any more than 1 hour before serving.

pepper-crusted maple-glazed salmon

serves 4

If you make only one recipe from this book, let this be the one. The deceptively easy yet indescribably delicious maple-soy marinade creates a candied salmon fillet that melts in your mouth, while the black pepper crust provides the perfect savory foil. Even people who don't like fish become devoted converts after one bite. The closely guarded recipe was divulged to me—after several hours on the torture rack—by Andrew Zimbel, owner of The Amazing Food Service in Toronto. Such a big payoff for so little effort. Now *that's* amazing.

3/4	cup maple syrup (see page 135)
1/4	cup soy sauce
4	(6-ounce) salmon fillets, *skin removed*
1/4	cup coarsely ground black pepper (Grind it yourself, or purchase "cracked" pepper at your grocery store.)
1/2	teaspoon peanut (or other vegetable) oil, or a spritz of oil spray

1 In a small deep bowl, or a plastic bag, mix maple syrup and soy sauce. Arrange fillets so that marinade completely covers fish. Marinate in the refrigerator for as long as possible (a minimum of 4 hours, but ideally 24 hours to do it justice). Turn salmon every few hours.

2 Preheat oven to 500°F.

3 Rub oil on a 10 x 10-inch sheet of aluminum foil.

4 Place pepper on a small plate. Remove salmon from marinade and pat top side only into cracked pepper to coat. Place fillets, pepper side up, on foil.

5 Bake on the top rack of the oven for 7 minutes. (Syrup may cause fish to smoke when cooking—don't be alarmed.) Salmon can also be grilled directly over hot coals for about 3 minutes per side. Don't even think about using a microwave. Avoid overcooking the fillets. Salmon is best when the color has turned to a pale pink, but the fish is still moist throughout. Serve immediately on warmed plates.

le secret The longer the salmon marinates (up to 48 hours) the better it is.

note When multiplying the recipe for larger groups, it is not necessary to increase the marinade proportionately. Just mix enough marinade (in the same 3 parts maple syrup to 1 part soy sauce proportions) to cover all the fillets.

tips for advance prep Although the fish can be placed in its marinade up to 48 hours in advance, it should only be peppered and cooked just before serving.

(i can't believe it's not) creamed corn

serves 4

This corn recipe was born to accompany the maple salmon, but it will also add life to an infinite number of dishes. The first time I tasted it (at the now-defunct L.A. restaurant Modada), I was sucked in by its sweetness. Talking my way into the kitchen, I asked the chef what made his creamed corn so special. I assumed his answer would include heavy cream and lots of butter. To my surprise, he told me it contained nothing more than fresh corn and a pinch of salt and pepper. The secret rests in separating the sweet milk and meat of the corn kernels from their less-tasty casings instead of simply cutting the kernels from the cob. I do add some butter (because, as the ads say, "butter makes it better") and a bit of chipotle powder, but neither is necessary.

8	ears of corn, *husked*
2	tablespoons butter (optional)
1/4	teaspoon chipotle chili powder (optional; see page 134)
	salt and freshly ground pepper to taste

1 Using a sharp paring knife, start at the top of the cob and score the middle of each row of kernels. The object here is to puncture the individual casings so that it is easier to force out the contents (as described in step 2). The depth of the incision, as well as your ability to slice a straight line, is of no consequence.

2 Grab your largest pot and a common dinner knife. Hold the cob inside the pot. Starting at the top of the cob, run the back side of the blade down the cob, using pressure to force out the meat and milk from the casings. Be forewarned, this is a messy job (hence the pot) that requires a healthy amount of muscle power. If possible, do this outdoors.

3 Discard the cobs and transfer the corn mash to a smaller pot. If you decide to add butter and chipotle, do it here. Warm over medium heat for a few watchful minutes, stirring frequently. If you warm corn for too long, or over too high a temperature, the natural liquids will evaporate and the corn will become gooey.

4 Season with salt and pepper, and serve immediately.

le secret The fresher and sweeter the corn, the better the mash.

tips for advance prep Corn can be prepped earlier in the day and refrigerated. Warm just before serving.

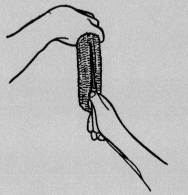
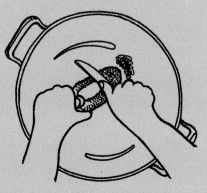

grilled raisin bread, stilton & pear dessertwich

serves 4

Fred Eric, the purple-haired bad boy of the L.A. restaurant scene, helped me add a playful twist to the classic combination of Stilton and pears.

1	tablespoon butter
1	ripe pear, *peeled, cored, and sliced thinly* (If a ripe pear cannot be found, sauté slices in a tablespoon of butter over medium heat for 5 minutes or until tender, or use canned pears.)
3	ounces Stilton cheese, *sliced or crumbled finely*
4	slices raisin bread (ideally, cinnamon raisin)

1 Divide ingredients in half and assemble two pear-and-Stilton "sandwiches."
2 Melt butter in a sauté pan over medium heat.
3 When butter is fully melted, place both sandwiches in pan, cover, and grill for 2 minutes per side, or until browned like a conventional grilled-cheese sandwich.
4 Remove from pan and slice each sandwich diagonally into four triangles. Serve immediately (ideally with the Adventure Club accompaniment).

le secret Keep a watchful eye on the pan when grilling the dessertwich; raisin bread will begin to burn only moments after it is browned to perfection.
the adventure club Break out the port.
the even easier way out Serve Stilton and pears with Carr's wheatmeal crackers.

the grill of ecstasy

the grill of ecstasy

★ sidesaddle ★ chipotle dry-rub shrimp with cilantro dipping sauce ★ love me tenderloin ★ grilled asparagus spears ★ ★ psychedelic coleslaw ★ grilled fruit kabobs ★

dinner for 4

This meal would max out your credit card in a swanky restaurant. But in your own backyard, by the glow of the BBQ, it's an affordable luxury.

suggested running order for advance prep
1 shell, clean, and devein shrimp 2 prepare dry rub for shrimp and toss with shrimp 3 prepare dry rub for meat and rub down meat 4 make coleslaw 5 trim and peel asparagus 6 make cilantro sauce for shrimp 7 cut fruit and assemble fruit kabobs (unless you are letting guests assemble their own) 8 squeeze lime juice 9 start grill

total advance prep time 1 hour, 20 minutes

suggested running order for cooking once the guests have arrived
1 make cocktail 2 grill shrimp 3 grill meat 4 remove cooked meat from grill, cover with aluminum foil for 5 minutes while you grill asparagus 5 assemble plates and serve 6 grill kabobs

total grill duty once guests have arrived 1 hour, with plenty of time off

music to cook by Lyle Lovett. *The Road to Encinada.* Pure insightful Lyle.

music to dine by Gene Autry. *The Essential Gene Autry.* Classic cowboy tunes from the singing cowboy.

music to wash by Lucinda Williams. *Car Wheels on a Gravel Road.* An overlooked "alternative country" artist who finally earned some well-deserved mainstream exposure with this Grammy-winning album.

recommended wine California Zinfandel or a Chilean Cabernet. The chili-rubbed tenderloin begs for a big spicy red to temper its fire.

sidesaddle

serves 4

Cognac usually brings to mind fireplaces and cold winter nights. But ice it with a squeeze of lime and a splash of Cointreau and it becomes the perfect summer cocktail.

1   lime
1/4 cup granulated sugar,
     placed on a small saucer
4   ounces Cognac (When blending
     cocktails, use V.S. Cognac,
     the youngest, least expensive
     category.)
2   ounces Cointreau, or triple sec
4   tablespoons freshly squeezed
     lime juice
2   cups ice

1   Use a lime wedge to moisten the rims of four
     martini-style glasses. Turn the glass upside
     down and press into the sugar to coat.
     Shake off excess.

2   Fill a martini shaker or a large
     glass with ice. Add the Cognac,
     Cointreau, and lime juice and
     shake or stir. Strain into the
     sugar-rimmed glasses.
     Garnish with lime twist.

chipotle dry-rub shrimp with cilantro dipping sauce

serves 4

Every time I pan-cook these shrimp indoors, I set off the smoke alarm. It's a ringing affirmation that I have hit the crowd-pleasing jackpot. Whether they are cooked on the stove or an outdoor grill, they always disappear instantly. XL shrimp are a bit pricey, but a couple of these memorably seasoned shellfish per person is all it takes to impress. The recipe multiplies effortlessly to create a winning appetizer for any size dinner or cocktail party.

chipotle dry-rub shrimp

3/4	pound uncooked 12/15 count shrimp (translation: 12 to 15 shrimp to a pound)
1	tablespoon dried oregano
1/2	tablespoon dried thyme
1	teaspoon lemon pepper (a mixed spice seasoning), or dried lemon peel
1/4–1/2	teaspoon ground chipotle chili (may be replaced with cayenne pepper, but only after you've been to hell and back searching for chipotle; see page 134)
1/2	teaspoon salt
1/2	teaspoon freshly ground black pepper
1	tablespoon olive oil

1 Shell and devein shrimp (see page 140). I leave the tails on for esthetic reasons. Pat dry.
2 In a medium-size bowl, mix all spices. Add shrimp and toss thoroughly.
3 Grill for 2 minutes per side, or until shrimp are no longer translucent. Brush both sides lightly with olive oil while cooking. Do not overcook. Serve hot, or at room temperature, with cilantro dipping sauce.

cilantro dipping sauce

1	cup lightly packed fresh cilantro leaves, *stems discarded before measuring*
3	tablespoons freshly squeezed lime juice
1/2	cup sour cream

1 Blend cilantro and lime juice in a food processor or blender until cilantro is liquefied. Pour into a small bowl and stir in sour cream. Refrigerate until ready for use.

le secret The chipotle chili does all the hard work by adding a unique smoky flavor to the shrimp.
the adventure club Serve shrimp "on the bar-b" (see page 76).
alarming advice Unhook your smoke alarm before cooking shrimp (but don't forget to reconnect it).
alternate pan method Heat a well-seasoned iron skillet (see page 129) or nonstick pan over high heat. When pan is smoking hot, add several drops of oil. Then add as many shrimp as pan can accommodate without overlapping. Cook for 1 1/2 minutes per side, or until no longer translucent. Do not overcook. Repeat as necessary to cook all shrimp.
specialized cooking apparatus food processor or blender; brush
tips for advanced prep The dry rub can be made ahead and stored in a sealed jar. Make extra; it lasts almost indefinitely. The shrimp can be shelled and deveined up to a day in advance.

love me tenderloin

This chili-rubbed fillet puts up a hot and fiery front that will tease your tongue. But deep down lies a sweet and tender soul that will melt in your mouth.

2	tablespoons New Mexican (or any other) chili powder
1	tablespoon chipotle chili powder (if available, or 1 additional tablespoon New Mexican chili powder)
1	tablespoon freshly ground black pepper
2	tablespoons granulated sugar
1	(2-pound) fillet beef tenderloin, *whole* (cut from the large end, which should be approximately 4 inches in diameter)
1	tablespoon salt

1 In a medium-size bowl, combine chili powders, black pepper, and sugar.
2 Generously coat and pat down tenderloin with rub mixture. Wrap in waxed paper or plastic wrap and let sit at room temperature for 30 minutes.
3 If using a charcoal BBQ, arrange a generous amount of coals on one side of the grill. For propane grills, light one side only.
4 Wait until coals are red-hot and a light layer of gray ash has formed overtop. Just before grilling, pat down tenderloin with salt. Cook meat for 3 minutes directly over the hot coals. Then rotate 1/4 turn and cook for another 3 minutes. Follow the same procedure for the remaining 2 sides. When all sides have been seared (and probably blackened), transfer meat to the side of the grill where it is not directly over any hot coals. Cover grill and cook for 15 to 20 more minutes, turning once, or until fillet has reached your desired degree of doneness.
5 Place meat on a plate and cover with aluminum foil. Let sit for 5 minutes before slicing.

le secret Don't be afraid to let the meat char on the outside when grilling it. It's essential to the flavor.
tips for advance prep The meat can be left in its dry rub for up to a day in the refrigerator.
shopping tip Even though smaller precut pieces of tenderloin are available in the meat section of most grocery stores, the large cut required for this recipe will need to be specially prepared by a butcher. Don't be shocked when you see the price per pound (about fifteen dollars). I promise you, it will be well worth it.
specialized cooking apparatus grill
alternative cooking method During the off-season, tenderloin can be cooked indoors. Sear in a very hot well-seasoned skillet for a total of 5 minutes (rotating 1/4 turn every minute or so), then finish in a preheated 350°F oven for 20 to 25 minutes, or until meat has reached your desired degree of doneness.

grilled asparagus spears

serves 4

Grilling asparagus miraculously transforms it from the kind of vegetable you hated as a kid to a sweet, meaty, lip-smackin' treat that you can't get enough of as an adult. This is the least amount of work you will ever have to do to be considered a saint among BBQers.

1	pound fresh asparagus (Look for thick firm stalks with firm, deep green or purplish tips. Also check the bottom of the spears. If they are dried up, chances are they have been sitting around for a while.)
4	tablespoons olive oil
1	teaspoon salt (This may seem like a lot—just trust me.)

1 Trim off the tough bottom of the spear by grasping each end and bending it gently until it snaps at its natural point of tenderness—usually two-thirds of the way down the spear. If the spear is less than 6 inches long, chances are it has already been trimmed for you. Then take a vegetable peeler and peel off the outer skin of the lower half of the remaining stalk.

2 Place asparagus on a plate. Drizzle oil overtop and turn spears until they are coated. Sprinkle with salt and turn again.

3 Grill asparagus for 5 minutes over a hot grill. Each minute or so, roll each spear $1/4$ turn. Asparagus should begin to brown in spots (indicating that its natural sugars are caramelizing) but should not be allowed to char. Dripping oil may cause flare-ups. Keep a glass or spray bottle of water handy to spritz on coals if necessary.

4 Remove from grill and serve (eating spears with your fingers enhances the experience).

le secret Thicker spears fare better on the grill.

the adventure club Wrap grilled spears with slices of prosciutto (see page 135)—a perfect appetizer for your next cocktail party.

specialized cooking apparatus grill

tips for advance prep Spears can be trimmed and peeled earlier in the day. Refrigerate, standing asparagus upright in an inch of water.

psychedelic coleslaw

serves 4

Picture yourself at the grill in the backyard, with sesame dreams and honeydew skies. Suddenly someone appears with the coleslaw, the girl with kaleidoscope eyes. This recipe takes the notion of coleslaw and fuses it with Far Eastern flavors. The fluorescent colors will make you think you are having a flashback—even if you never turned on, tuned in, or dropped out.

1/4	cup rice wine vinegar
2	teaspoons toasted sesame oil
2	teaspoons freshly squeezed lime juice
1	tablespoon honey
1/4	teaspoon cayenne pepper (Optional; this meal already has lots of spice, so you might want to lay off it in this recipe. However, if you are serving psychedelic coleslaw with any other meal, the cayenne provides a nice kick.)
2	tablespoons sesame seeds
2	carrots, *peeled and grated coarsely*
1/3	head red cabbage (looks purple to me), *cored, then cut crosswise into the narrowest ribbons possible, then separated*
1	yellow bell pepper, *seeds and membranes removed, then sliced lengthwise into the thinnest strips possible*
1	red bell pepper, *seeds and membranes removed, then sliced lengthwise into the thinnest strips possible*
1/2	medium-size sweet onion, *finely sliced, rings separated*
1 1/2	tablespoons finely grated or minced fresh gingerroot, *peeled first*
1	cup lightly packed cilantro leaves, *stems discarded before measuring, chopped*
1/4	daikon—a large white Japanese radish (optional; available in some grocery stores), *peeled and grated coarsely*

1 In a small bowl whisk together vinegar, sesame oil, lime juice, honey, and cayenne. Set aside.
2 Toast sesame seeds in a dry pan over medium heat for 3 minutes, or until lightly browned.
3 In a large bowl, combine remaining ingredients and toss thoroughly. Then toss with dressing. Serve immediately or refrigerate.
4 Just before serving, toss with sesame seeds (reserving a few to sprinkle overtop).

le secret Do not prepare more than a couple of hours in advance because the color of the cabbage will seep into the other ingredients.
the adventure club Add a teaspoon of dried wasabi, or 1/4 teaspoon wasabi paste, to dressing in step 1 (blend thoroughly with a whisk).
tips for advance prep Vegetables and dressing can be prepared earlier in the day. Store red cabbage separately and don't mix veggies with the dressing until just before serving.
specialized cooking apparatus a very sharp, large knife

grilled fruit kabobs

serves 4

Prepare these in advance, or set out cut fruit in bowls along with some skewers and encourage guests to assemble their own kabobs.

Select some or all of the following fresh fruits:

$1/2$	**pineapple,** *outer rind and core discarded, cut into 1-inch cubes*
1	**mango,** *skin and pit discarded, cut into 1-inch cubes*
1	**peach,** *skin on, pitted, cut into 1-inch pieces*
1	**banana,** *peel on, cut into $1/2$-inch slices*
8	**strawberries,** *stems removed*
8	**seedless grapes (whole)**
$1/4$	**cup granulated sugar**
2	**tablespoons vegetable oil** (to coat grill and prevent stickage)
1	**pint ice cream** (optional)
4	**bamboo skewers,** *soaked in water for 30 minutes,* **or metal skewers**

1 Skewer fruit and sprinkle generously with sugar.
2 Rub down grill grate with a rag dipped in the oil. Then grill kabobs for 8 minutes directly over hot coals, rotating $1/4$ turn every 2 minutes or so, or until fruit starts to caramelize and brown slightly. Serve as is or over ice cream.

specialized cooking apparatus bamboo or metal skewers; grill
the even easier way out Give every guest a stick and a handful of marshmallows.

guerriller tactics

Grilling isn't exactly an exact science. Here are a few tips culled from my personal experiences that should help smooth the way.

- If you intend to BBQ on the same day you purchase a new grill, allow one hour of assembly time for each language that the instruction manual is written in.

- When using a charcoal grill, start the fire early to avoid the public humiliation of famished dinner guests watching you madly fan the uncooperative coals.

- When using a propane grill, remember that the probability that your rusty gas gauge is stuck at "full" directly correlates to the number of guests you are trying to impress with your grilling prowess.

- The more sophisticated your guests are, the more eager they will be to toast marshmallows (or s'mores, if they attended summer camp) for dessert.

- Be forewarned that "I brought a little blush wine that's perfect for barbecues" is a euphemism for "Someone gave me this bottle and I would never lower myself to opening it in my house." Save it for the return invitation.

citrus circus

citrus circus

★ **mighty lemon drop** ★ **citrus tapenade** ★ **lemon-herb-roasted rock cornish hens, stuffed with whipped yams, on a nest of string beans** ★ **blood orange granita** ★

dinner for 4

If life hands you lemons, juggle them. Most of the components of this meal are infused with the zesty essence of citrus fruits. The bright flavors and colorful presentation will turn even the sourest day into a three-ring circus.

suggested running order for advance prep
1 start granita 2 bake yams 3 squeeze lemon juice and prepare simple syrup for lemon drops 4 make tapenade and toast crostini 5 trim string beans 6 prepare hens 7 whip yams

total advance prep time 2 hours, with some time off for good behavior while you are waiting for the yams to finish baking

suggested running order for cooking once the guests have arrived
1 preheat oven 2 make cocktail 3 serve tapenade 4 put hens in the oven 5 remove hens when they are done, cover with aluminum foil 6 reheat yams 7 steam beans 8 arrange beans on plates, remove lemon from hens, and use a soupspoon to stuff their cavities with yams. Rest each hen on a nest of beans and serve 9 serve granita

total kitchen duty after guests have arrived 40 minutes

music to cook by XTC. *Oranges and Lemons*. Literate deconstruction of the British Invasion.

music to dine by Cirque du Soleil. *Alegria*. Soaring vocals atop inspired musique, as featured in the circus production.

music to wash by Fatboy Slim. *You've Come a Long Way, Baby*. Cool samples, phat hooks, and an upbeat vibe.

recommended wine California Sauvignon Blanc. The natural acidity and citrus bouquet of this wine are a good balance for the dominant lemon essence of the chicken.

mighty lemon drop

serves 4

Contemporary martinis have little in common with their namesake other than their moniker. The new concoctions are really bastardized cocktails, mixed in martini shakers and strained into martini glasses. But who cares? Traditional martinis are simply a ploy for grown-ups to drink gin straight from the bottle—not that I deny them that right. Well-conceived modern martinis blend a generous portion of distilled grains with bright concentrated flavors such as Cointreau and fresh citrus juice. The lemon drop is one of the enduring survivors of that trend. It's lemonade for consenting adults, with no pretense other than good taste.

6   ounces lemon-flavored vodka (a.k.a. Citron)
2   ounces Cointreau, or triple sec
4   tablespoons freshly squeezed lemon juice
2   teaspoons simple syrup (see page 139), or to taste
2   cups ice
1   lemon or 4 candy lemon drops (for garnish)

1   Fill a martini shaker or a large glass with ice. Add vodka, Cointreau, lemon juice, and simple syrup and shake or stir. Strain into chilled martini glasses. Garnish with a candy lemon drop or a lemon twist.

le secret Lemons vary in their degree of tartness. Taste the mix before adding simple syrup to determine how much is required. **warning** This cocktail is deceptively strong. Pace yourself and your guests accordingly.

citrus tapenade

serves 4

This orange twist on the classic French tapenade (a.k.a. black olive paste) is rich, zesty, and aromatic—just as a stimulating dinner guest should be. It's perfect for dinner parties because the flavors improve when it is made ahead of time.

1	cup black kalamata olives, *pitted. Discard any mushy olives.* (Other types of black olives may be used, but stay away from the common colossal black olive. For the freshest olives at the lowest price, visit a Greek or Middle Eastern market.)
1	medium-size orange, *zested (see page 140). Use only the zest.*
1/2	lemon, *zested. Use only the zest.*
1	clove garlic, *minced*
1/4	teaspoon red pepper flakes
1/2	teaspoon fennel or anise seeds
1/2	teaspoon freshly ground black pepper
3/4	cup lightly packed fresh Italian parsley, *stems discarded before measuring, chopped coarsely*
1	tablespoon fresh rosemary, *stems discarded before measuring*
1	tablespoon olive oil
1/2	thin sourdough baguette, or rustic crackers or bagel chips

1 Dump all of the ingredients, except the bread, into a food processor and puree. If you are using a blender to puree, you may need to add some extra oil to facilitate blending. After blending, place in a bowl. Excess oil will rise to the edges of the bowl. Drain off.
2 Make crostini by cutting baguette into thin slices and toasting in a toaster or oven.
3 Spread tapenade on crisps just before serving, or let guests do it themselves.

le secret Stay focused when pitting the olives. The pits have an uncanny ability to sneak out of the pit pile back into the "finished" mound. If you are not vigilant, you will discover this when you hear a wayward pit pinging off the blade of the food processor.
the adventure club Serve in a hollowed-out orange.
specialized cooking apparatus food processor or blender; grater or zester
tips for advance prep Tapenade can be made up to 2 days in advance and refrigerated. Let warm to room temperature before serving.

lemon-herb-roasted rock cornish hens

serves 4

I used to shy away from Cornish hens because I equated them with brown plaid, shag carpets, and '70s dinner parties. Then recently, I was looking for an offbeat way to serve something "chickeny" and I decided to wing it. After all, if Blondie and Cher can make comebacks, these hens deserve another chance to rock. To my surprise, I was pleasantly reminded of why these diminutive birds were so popular to begin with. Perched on a "nest" of string beans and stuffed with my whipped yams, they look festive and, dare I say . . . very contemporary.

4	(1¹/2-pound) Cornish hens, *thawed overnight in the refrigerator, if frozen*
3	tablespoons salt
6	tablespoons butter, *at room temperature*
1	tablespoon freshly ground black pepper
3	tablespoons fresh rosemary, *stems discarded before measuring, chopped finely*
4	cloves garlic, *minced*
1	lemon, *zested (see page 140), then quartered*

1 Arrange oven racks so that the birds can be put in the center of the oven. Preheat oven to 475°F.
2 Discard giblets (and any other foreign objects) that you find inside the birds. Rinse birds under cold water, then pat dry. Rub generously with salt, inside and out.
3 Blend butter, pepper, rosemary, garlic, and lemon zest in a small bowl. Rub the mixture all over the birds. Use your fingers to separate the skin from the breast meat and slide some of the mixture underneath the skin. Then stuff a quarter lemon into the cavity of each bird. Cross the legs and bind with twine.
4 Place the birds, breast side up, in a large, shallow roasting pan or some facsimile thereof, and bake for 25 minutes. Then remove to baste. When you return the pan to the oven, rotate it 180 degrees from its original position (this compensates for the uneven distribution of heat in most ovens). Cook for 20 more minutes, or until the juices of the thigh meat run clear when pricked.
5 Remove hens from oven, cover tightly with aluminum foil, and let sit at room temperature for 5 minutes before serving (this locks in the juices). Cut twine, remove lemon quarters from the cavities, stuff with whipped yams, and serve immediately on warmed plates.

le secret Select birds of equal weight so that they finish cooking at the same time.
the adventure club Place 3 cooked quail eggs in the nest under each bird.
notes i) Roasting is not an exact science. Some birds just take longer than others (and some ovens may not be the exact temperature they indicate). ii) Rock Cornish hens usually come frozen (at approximately four dollars each). The best way to thaw them is to transfer them from the freezer to the fridge the night before you intend to cook them.
warning The hen drippings and melted butter will create a substantial pool of fat in the bottom of the pan. My singed arm hairs are a testimony to the fact that these drippings can easily ignite if spilled in a gas oven.
specialized cooking apparatus roasting pan; 3 feet of natural fiber mailing-type twine
tips for advance prep Hens can be fully prepped earlier in the day and refrigerated.

whipped yams

The yam marketing council should hire a new publicist. What else can explain the relative obscurity of this noble, nutritious vegetable (save for its fifteen minutes of fame on Thanksgiving Day)? Unlike regular potatoes, which remain starchy, the yam contains an enzyme that converts most of its starch to sugar as it matures. These natural sugars caramelize when yams are baked, making this one dish that is easy to pitch.

4	medium-size yams
1/2	cup half-and-half, or whole milk
1/4	teaspoon freshly grated nutmeg, or cinnamon, or chipotle powder

1 Preheat oven to 400°F. Bake yams on a sheet of aluminum foil for 1 1/2 hours, or until they are soft and have started to ooze beads of dark syrup.
2 Remove yams from oven and allow to cool slightly. Then separate and discard the skins.
3 Whip yams in a food processor or mash by hand. (Unlike regular mashed potatoes, yams benefit from the smoothness created by a food processor.) Add nutmeg and slowly mix in cream.

le secret Bake the yams for longer than feels appropriate.
specialized cooking apparatus food processor or hand masher
tips for advanced prep Yams can be made earlier in the day and reheated over low heat.

string beans tossed in browned butter

The beans here are more of a colorful vegetable garnish than a stand-alone recipe. That's still no excuse to overcook them.

1 1/2	pounds string beans, *stems trimmed*
2	tablespoons butter, *at room temperature*
2	tablespoons freshly squeezed lemon juice
	salt and freshly ground pepper to taste

1 Fill a large pot with two inches of water and place a steamer inside. Bring water to a boil. Add beans and cover for 5 minutes, or until beans are cooked throughout but still crisp to the bite. If you don't have a steamer, boil beans in boiling water.
2 Thoroughly drain water, then return beans to the emptied pot. Let beans sit, uncovered, for 2 minutes so that any water coating them has evaporated. Pour out any accumulated water.
3 Melt butter in a saucepan over medium heat. Cook for 3 minutes, or until melted butter has turned golden brown (this adds a slightly nutty flavor). Remove from heat; add lemon juice, and pour over beans. Sprinkle with salt and pepper, and toss thoroughly.

specialized cooking apparatus vegetable steamer
tips for advance prep Beans can be trimmed earlier in the day and refrigerated in a bowl of water.

blood orange granita

serves 4

Granita is a delicate form of Italian ice made from freshly squeezed fruit juice and sugar. It is often served as a palate cleanser between courses in swish restaurants. Despite its noble function, it is ludicrously simple to prepare at home. When served in larger portions, the deep color and pure fruit flavor make it an elegant and refreshing dessert.

2	cups freshly squeezed blood orange juice, *room temperature* (Blood oranges look like regular oranges on the outside, but their flesh and juice are deep red. This exotic fruit can be difficult to find—but it is worth a try. If they are nowhere to be found, replace with freshly squeezed orange, pink grapefruit, or lemon juice.)
1/3	cup granulated sugar (Adjust sweetness for the alternative juices by letting sugar dissolve in juice, then adding more sugar, if necessary, until the juice has the sweetness of a sugary fruit drink.)
4	sprigs mint (optional)

1 Add sugar to orange juice and let sit for 2 minutes. Stir well, then pour into an 8 x 10-inch cake pan or Tupperware-type container until juice is half an inch deep. Place in freezer. At the same time, put four martini or small wine glasses in the freezer to chill.

2 After an hour, remove pan from freezer and use a fork to mix the frozen bits with the unfrozen liquid. Return to freezer.

3 Repeat the process an hour later, using the fork to break up the hardening ice formation. Return to freezer for one more hour.

4 Use fork to stir up and mash the solid ice into crystals. Serve in the chilled glasses. Top with a mint sprig, and serve with gingersnaps or fancy Pepperidge Farm–type cookies.

the even easier way out Serve store-bought orange sorbet and cookies.

tips for advance prep Can (and should) be made earlier in the day, or the day before.

breakfast anytime

★ gonzo grapefruit ★ eggs carbonara ★ blackened home-fried
potatoes from hell ★ the perfect cup of coffee ★

breakfast for 4

After many years of chasing all over town for the perfect morning meal, I have concluded that if you want something made to your own dictatorial standards, make it yourself. Now, every Sunday morning, I kneel religiously before the stands at my local farmers market, then race home and get crackin'. What follows is my ultimate post-market brunch. If you sleep through your alarm, don't worry; it's just as good for dinner.

suggested running order for advance prep
1 boil potatoes 2 prep fixin's for home fries 3 cook pancetta
4 prep fixin's for eggs 5 cut and segment grapefruit
6 start home fries 20 minutes ahead of your guests' arrival

total advance prep time 1 hour, 15 minutes

suggested running order for cooking once the guests have arrived
1 boil water 2 make coffee 3 make grapefruit
4 when potatoes are nearing completion, make eggs 5 make toast

total kitchen duty after guests have arrived 20 minutes

music to cook by Henry Mancini. *Breakfast at Tiffany's: Music from the Motion Picture Score.* The next best thing to having breakfast with Audrey herself.

music to dine by Vince Guaraldi. *Oh, Good Grief!* The electric harpsichord–laden themes to the beloved "Peanuts" cartoons.

music to wash by Renee Fleming. *The Beautiful Voice.* When you call your album this, you'd better be exceptional. And she is.

gonzo grapefruit
serves 4

Hey, it's 5 o'clock somewhere.

2	whole grapefruits (pink if available), *sliced in half*
4	ounces vodka (strictly optional, but you know Hunter S. Thompson would have it this way)
6	teaspoons brown sugar

1 Set one oven rack on the highest level, then preheat broiler.
2 Using a small serrated knife, cut around grapefruit to separate the fruit from the skin and the segments from each other (just like your mother did for you). Pour out a bit of the grapefruit juice to make room for the vodka.
3 Drizzle 1 ounce of vodka over each grapefruit half and let it seep between the slices (I doubt your mother did *this* for you).
4 Immediately before broiling, sprinkle $1^1/2$ teaspoons of sugar overtop of each half.
5 Place grapefruit on rack so that the top is 3 inches below the broiler and broil for 3 minutes. Garnish with a raspberry or strawberry, if available. Serve immediately.

le secret Don't eat your grapefruit this way every day.
tips for advance prep Grapefruit can be cut a few hours in advance. Don't sprinkle sugar until just before broiling.

eggs carbonara

serves 4

What can I say? I am a creature of habit. In restaurants, when I find something I like, I tend to stick with it—forever. After a while I become so familiar with the dish that I can tell when the chef takes a day off. So you can imagine my dismay when I walked into Hugo's (an entertainment industry haunt in West Hollywood that I used to frequent on Saturday mornings) and discovered they had taken their famous Eggs Carbonara off the menu. These eggs were as close as any restaurant has come to a perfect breakfast. They were a kitchen-sink cacophony of spicy pancetta, scallions, garlic—and whatever else didn't make it into the pasta the night before. Instead of burying the flavorful ingredients in a fluffy omelette, the whole mess was scrambled. No fuss, no muss—all flavor. This recipe is based on my loose interpretation of the original, with an extra helping of all the good stuff.

8	eggs
	salt and lots of freshly ground black pepper to taste
1/2	cup freshly grated Parmigiano-Reggiano (see page 135)
2	tablespoons milk or water
1/2	pound pancetta (see page 135), or thickly sliced bacon, *sliced crosswise into 1/4-inch strips*
1 1/2	tablespoons olive oil
6	scallions, *finely chopped*
1	jalapeño or serrano chili, *minced*
5	garlic cloves, *minced* (optional)
1	cup fresh cilantro, or Italian parsley, *stems discarded before measuring*
1	ripe avocado (optional), *skin and pit removed, then diced into 1/4-inch cubes*
	bread for toast (you are on your own here)

1 In a bowl, beat eggs, salt, black pepper, cheese, and milk. Set aside.
2 Cook pancetta in a sauté pan over medium-high heat, stirring occasionally until it is done like crisp pieces of bacon. Drain on a paper towel.
3 Discard the fat from the sauté pan and use a paper towel to wipe it down. Add oil, scallions, jalapeño, and garlic to the pan, and cook over medium-high heat for 2 to 3 minutes, or until garlic shows the first sign of turning golden.
4 Add cilantro, avocado, and cooked pancetta. Stir for 2 more minutes.
5 Reduce heat to medium, add egg mixture to pan, and stir until eggs are cooked to your liking. Serve immediately on warmed plates.

le secret The richness of the parmesan cheese gives the eggs an unexpectedly sweet flavor.
tips for advanced prep Nothing in this recipe should be prepared too far in advance.

blackened home-fried potatoes from hell

serves 4

In my quest for the perfect breakfast combo, potatoes were always a disappointment. Whenever I saw home fries or hash browns on the menu of a breakfast joint, my mind would conjure up a plate of crispy, browned potatoes, full of texture and flavor. Inevitably my eggs arrived with a mound of snow-white mealy spuds, offering only a teasing hint of the crispiness I yearned for. If they had any color at all, it was usually due to a deceptive dusting of paprika. Making crispy home fries takes a lot of patience and surface space—which is exactly why most busy restaurants are incapable of satisfying my craving. The beauty of cooking home fries at *home* is that you can brown them to your heart's content.

2	pounds potatoes (Yukon gold, white, or red potatoes are best, but russet or baking potatoes work well, too.)
too much	butter
too much	olive oil
6	cloves garlic, *diced*
1	medium-size cooking onion, *diced*
1/2	cup fresh rosemary, thyme, or dill, *stems discarded before measuring*
	salt and freshly ground black pepper to taste

1 Quarter potatoes, skin on, and boil them in eight cups of water with a teaspoon of salt for approximately 20 minutes, or until tender to the poke of a fork. Drain water.

2 In your best large nonstick pan or well-seasoned skillet, over medium-high heat, add 1 tablespoon butter and 1 tablespoon olive oil. When the butter/oil mixture is hot, transfer potatoes to pan and use a spatula to chop the quarters into smaller pieces (there is no science here). As the potatoes absorb the butter and oil during cooking, continue to add in equal amounts, as required, to keep the pan well greased. Sauté for 20 minutes, turning occasionally, or until potatoes begin browning on all sides. If the potatoes start burning before they brown, reduce the heat.

3 Add garlic and onions and continue cooking for 15 more minutes, or until potatoes, garlic, and onions are all very browned and crispy.

4 When potatoes are almost done to your liking, add herbs, salt, and pepper to taste. Cook for a few more minutes, then serve immediately on warmed plates.

le secret It's all in the timing of adding the garlic and onions (which can really be learned only through trial and error). Adding them too soon will cause them to burn before the potatoes are crisp, and too late will prevent the garlic and onion from fully caramelizing.

specialized cooking apparatus nonstick pan or very well-seasoned skillet

tips for advanced prep Potatoes can be boiled, or baked, up to a day in advance, and refrigerated.

the perfect cup of coffee

actually, 4 perfect cups

Good coffee is an equal-opportunity luxury. But not everybody seizes the opportunity. A perfect cup of coffee requires the harmonic convergence of several elements, the most important of which are the beans and the brewing method. Today's designer coffeemakers offer a plethora of space-age bells and whistles. Despite the technological advances of these units and their sleek lines, I am unwavering in my conviction that the most foolproof method for brewing full-bodied coffee is the humble French press (a.k.a. Bodum or plunger). This low-tech, low-cost (about twenty dollars) unit allows the coffee to steep, just like tea, thereby extracting every iota of flavor from each precious ground. More important, unlike traditional paper filters that absorb the coffee's natural oils, the mesh screen of a plunger keeps the oils where you want them—in your cup. Even old or inferior beans come to life when brewed in this manner. The end result is a potent cup of gloriously rich and thick coffee that will make you very, very happy.

6	tablespoons whole beans, or 5 tablespoons ground beans (This is more than most instructions specify. Fresh-roasted dark, oily beans—i.e., French, Italian, or espresso—are preferable.)
6	cups fresh cold water (Spring or filtered water is best. That said, I use tap water.)
1	(4-cup) French press

1 Bring water to a full rolling boil, then remove from heat immediately. Pour about half a cup of the boiling water into the plunger pot and a splash into each of the coffee mugs to heat them. This step is essential to avoid lukewarm coffee.

2 Grind beans. Conventional plunger wisdom calls for a coarse grind in order to keep the beans from escaping through the mesh screen. However, if you like your coffee thick and velvety, use a fine (i.e., espresso) grind. If you are using preground beans, buy them in quantities that will be consumed within a week.

3 Spoon ground coffee into plunger pot. (If you are half asleep, double-check that you have dumped out the warming water.) Add 4 cups of hot water and insert the plunger just far enough so that it acts like a lid. Let the coffee steep for 3 to 4 minutes, then press the plunger down very slowly and steadily. Allow another minute for the coffee sediment to settle to the bottom.

4 Hold the French press up to the sun before serving and pay homage to the coffee gods. If any hint of sunlight shines through the coffee, pour it out and start all over again.

le secret Store beans in a tightly sealed jar in your refrigerator.
the adventure club Steam your milk.
specialized cooking apparatus French press; coffee grinder

When your heart says indulge,
but your head says be sensible,
compromise with a granola parfait.
Layer alternate scoops of granola, yogurt,
fresh fruit, and (if desired) honey.

extreme cuisine

five dramatic cooking techniques

Since the release of my last book, *The Surreal Gourmet Entertains*, I have traveled the globe throwing spontaneous dinner parties wherever I could rustle up a kitchen and a willing audience. The hazard of having a good publicist, however, is that guests tend to arrive with impossibly high expectations. Instead of trying to compete with their fantasies, I counter with culinary theatrics from my Surreal bag of tricks. The ruse started at a dinner in Vienna where I poached salmon fillets in a dishwasher. The astonished reaction of my guests was all the encouragement I needed to begin experimenting with other techniques of urban legend. My kitchen at home began to resemble a mad laboratory as I pushed my household appliances well beyond the uses covered by their limited warranties. Despite some collateral damage, the process of testing and tweaking the following unconventional cooking methods was good fun and yielded results that surprised even me.

the fine print

If you play with fire (literally or figuratively) there is always the possibility that you may burn the joint down. All of the following methods have worked for me, but remember, I am a professional culinary adventurist. Proceed at your own risk, take proper precautions, and be forewarned: I have no liability insurance.

Poaching fish in the dishwasher is a virtually foolproof way to shock your friends, prepare a succulent meal, and do the dishes—all at the same time. I've poached salmon in more than a hundred dishwashers on three continents. There's never been a dull party.

the instruction manual

1 Seal individual-size fillets in aluminum foil (see page 140). DO NOT attempt to cook a whole fish.

2 Place fish packets on the top rack.

3 Add dirty dishes and lemon-scented soap. This optional step is not recommended for novices. However, as long as the salmon is tightly sealed in the aluminum foil, it will not absorb any soapy taste or smell.

4 Set the dishwasher to the "normal" cycle. Modern dishwashers have "economy" and "cool dry" settings, which are undesirable because they conserve heat. However, on the other end of the spectrum, the "pots and pans" setting tends to overcook the fish.

5 Run salmon through the entire wash-and-dry cycle—approximately 50 minutes for most models. I have poached salmon in almost every make and model, and although the temperatures and durations of the cycles vary with each machine, a little more or less "washing" will not affect it greatly because salmon is extremely forgiving.

6 To heighten the drama for your disbelieving guests—and to prove that you have nothing up your sleeve—let them crowd around the dishwasher when you load the salmon. When the cycle is complete, invite them back to witness the unloading.

7 Troubleshoot. The only time I ever had a problem was on live national TV. Five minutes before going on the air I learned that the heating element in the on-camera dishwasher was broken. After a quick huddle with the producer, I was forced to make the most of the situation by baking the salmon in the (gasp!) oven. To avoid this pedestrian fate, ask yourself the million-dollar question: When your dishwasher last completed its cycle, were the dishes hot? As long as the answer is yes, you are ready to poach.

dishwasher salmon with piquant dill sauce

serves 4

Set your doubts aside, put dinner in the dishwasher, and watch this multitasking kitchen appliance steal the show.

dishwasher salmon

1	tablespoon olive oil
4	(6-ounce) salmon fillets
4	tablespoons freshly squeezed lime juice
	salt and freshly ground black pepper to taste
	heavy-duty aluminum foil

1 Cut two 12-inch square sheets of aluminum foil.
2 Grease the shiny side of the foil with the oil. Place 2 fillets side by side on each square and fold up the outer edges.
3 Drizzle 1 tablespoon lime juice over each fillet. Season with salt and pepper.
4 Fold and pinch the aluminum foil extra tightly to create a watertight seal around each pair of fillets (see page 140). Make sure the packet is airtight by pressing down on it gently with your hand. If air escapes easily, rewrap.
5 Place foil packets on top rack of dishwasher. Run dishwasher for the entire "normal" cycle.
6 When cycle is complete, take out salmon, discard foil, place one fillet on each plate, and spoon a generous serving of piquant dill sauce overtop.

Don't have a dishwasher? Bake foil-wrapped packets in a preheated 400°F oven for 12 minutes.

piquant dill sauce

This bright, fresh-tasting sauce will add some bite to your catch.

1	tablespoon butter
2	leeks, white and pale green section only, *finely chopped, then thoroughly washed*
1	jalapeño chili, *seeds and membranes removed, finely diced*
2	garlic cloves, *minced*
1	cup chicken stock
1¹/₂	cups lightly packed fresh dill, *stems removed before measuring*
2	tablespoons freshly squeezed lemon juice
¹/₄	teaspoon salt
¹/₂	teaspoon freshly ground black pepper
3	tablespoons sour cream

1 Melt the butter over medium heat in a sauté pan.
2 Add the leeks, jalapeño, and garlic, and sauté for about 5 minutes, or until the leeks are translucent—but not brown.
3 Reduce heat to medium and add the stock. Simmer, uncovered, for 15 minutes. (Adjust heat as required to maintain simmer.) The liquid should reduce by half.

4 Remove from heat and let cool.
5 Transfer to a blender or food processor and add the dill, lemon juice, salt, and pepper. Puree until smooth. Reserve and reheat just before serving. Stir in the sour cream at the last minute.

le secret Make sure other items in the dishwasher, such as silverware, are securely stowed so that they do not fly around and pierce the foil packets.

music to poach by The Ventures. *Walk, Don't Run: The Best of the Ventures.* Domestic drudgery instantly transformed into beach party. Surf's up!

recommended wine Australian Chardonnay. Like a little thunder from down under, these big Chardonnays are well suited to fish dishes with creamy sauces.

drive it!

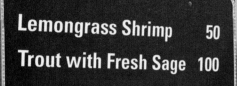

| Lemongrass Shrimp | 50 |
| Trout with Fresh Sage | 100 |

Ask someone to name the most unusual cooking method they can think of and the answer will probably be: cooking on a car engine. Ask them if they have ever tried it and the response is invariably "No . . . but I think someone wrote a book about it." That book is *Manifold Destiny* (Villard), the irreverent bible of engine cookery, written by Chris Maynard and Bill Scheller in 1989 and updated and reissued in 1998. Despite the fact that it never really jump-started a trend, it did succeed in entrenching the legend of car cookery in the public's mind.

I tracked down coauthor Bill Scheller, who was on the media circuit introducing his book to a new generation of highway cooks. As he was preparing to take a *People* magazine reporter for a drive—while cooking veal piccata—he enthusiastically addressed the most frequently asked questions. "Yes, the engine of a car is a safe and (relatively) clean place to cook. Yes, the food will smell and taste as good as if it was cooked in an oven—as long as the aluminum foil package is tightly sealed (although it braises rather than browns). Yes, all engines will do the trick, but older models make better ovens." As we talked, it occurred to me that engine cookery is just like funny-car racing—one part skill, one part novelty.

In keeping with my new credo that, with a little creativity, wine can be worked into every aspect of daily life, I mapped out a 140-mile drive to Santa Barbara's wine country. After concocting a few new recipes, I packed a cooler, enlisted a kindred spirit to navigate, and headed for Buellton, home of the tiny but noteworthy Sanford Winery.

After "preheating" the engine for twenty miles, I pulled over and threw dinner under the hood. Sixty miles of salivation later, I stopped to check the oven. My shrimp were still limp. Damn Honda for devising such efficient engines! Sensing that I was not using the hottest section, I lashed the packets against the exhaust manifold cover with aluminum foil bracing. The flesh of my fingertip sizzled as it accidentally touched the metal. (Hey, if you can't stand the heat, get off the road.) Twenty miles later, the intoxicating aroma of lemongrass began wafting into the passenger compartment. After arriving at the winery, I unlatched the hood and unpacked our "picnic" in front of several disbelieving tourists. The perfectly cooked fish and fragrant shrimp were a testament to the fact that anyone who can operate a motor vehicle can improve their standard of eating on the road.

the driver's manual*

1 In preparation for your first car meal, you should start by locating your engine's hot spots. Do this after any long drive by turning off the engine and letting the car sit for fifteen minutes. Then lift up the hood and quickly tap the various components of the engine block. On most vehicles, the hottest area is the exhaust manifold cover, but most engines have additional nooks and crannies that will generate enough heat to slow-cook your freeway fare. Stay clear of areas near any moving parts, such as the accelerator linkage, belts, or fans, and don't block any air intakes.

2 The sensible way (relatively speaking) to take advantage of the oven under your hood is to cook small portions of lightly textured foods. For this reason, fish is the perfect road chow. Before attempting any complex recipes, get to know your engine by cooking a hot dog (or tofu dog), the guinea pig of engine cooking—just don't forget the Grey Poupon.

3 When you are ready to cook:
- Layer 3 equal-size sheets of aluminum foil on top of each other. Treat as a single sheet.
- Grease the top sheet with a small amount of butter or olive oil to avoid stickage.
- Wrap ingredients in foil, then seal the seams by folding them over twice and tightly pinching them to create an airtight package (see page 140). FYI, even perfectly sealed packages will leak small amounts of liquid.

4 Before placing food on the engine, loosely roll up a 6-inch ball of foil, set it on top of the engine, and close the hood. Immediately reopen the hood and use the squashed ball to determine the amount of clearance space between the hood and the engine block. Set food on the predetermined sweet spot of your engine and secure it with a ball of foil that is equal to the clearance space less the pouch size. If you are cooking on a slanted section of the engine, strap the pouch in place with additional aluminum foil bracing.

5 Make, model, speed, outside temperature, food density, and placement will all affect the cooking time. Most small packets of food should cook in 1 to 2 hours. To ensure that you have fingers left to lick at the end of the meal, turn off the engine before loading, unloading, or checking.

6 The tool kit: a roll of aluminum foil; a roll of paper towels; an oven mitt; tongs for pulling food out of crevices; and forks, knives, and paper plates.

7 What would road food be without road music? Here are some great road discs:
- Booker T and The MGs. *Green Onions*
- Junior Brown. *Highway Patrol*
- AC/DC. *Highway to Hell*
- ZZ Top. *Eliminator*
- Bruce Springsteen. *Born to Run*
- Merle Haggard. *Lonesome Fugitive: The Merle Haggard Anthology*

Ladies and gentlemen, start your engines.

*This section was liberally pilfered from *Manifold Destiny* with permission from Bill Scheller.

six-cylinder lemongrass shrimp

serves 2 as an appetizer

These sweetly perfumed shrimp give a whole new meaning to the concept of Thai takeout.

1/2	pound uncooked 12/15 count shrimp, *shelled and deveined* (see page 140)
1	fresh lemongrass shoot, bottom 2 inches only, *sliced finely* (If lemongrass is unavailable, it may be replaced with 1 tablespoon of freshly minced gingerroot.)
1 1/2	tablespoons freshly squeezed lime juice
1/4	teaspoon salt
1	pinch cayenne pepper
2	tablespoons of fresh mint, *stems discarded before measuring, diced finely*
3	(12 x 12-inch) sheets of aluminum foil

1 Layer all three sheets of aluminum foil on top of one another and fold up the edges. Sprinkle lemongrass in the center. Place shrimp on top and drizzle with lime juice. Sprinkle with salt and cayenne, top with mint, and seal foil package (see page 140).
2 Place on engine, and cook for approximately 50 miles (80 km).
3 Open package and serve immediately. (Don't eat the lemongrass.)

Car's in the shop? Cook in a preheated 375°F oven for 10 minutes.

six-cylinder trout with fresh sage

serves 2 as a light meal

Whether you are on your way back from a country stream or your local grocery store, this recipe is bound to get you hooked on engine cooking.

1	whole trout (approximately 12 ounces), *gutted* salt and freshly ground pepper to taste
1	lemon, *sliced*
5	fresh whole sage leaves, or fresh dill sprigs
2	tablespoons butter, *sliced into 4 pieces*
3	(12 x 16-inch) sheets of aluminum foil

1 Layer all three sheets of aluminum foil on top of one another. Use one piece of the butter to grease the top layer.
2 Rinse trout and pat dry. Sprinkle inside with salt and pepper.
3 Line fish cavity with 3 lemon slices, sage, and remaining butter. Seal foil package (see page 140).
4 Place on engine and cook for approximately 100 miles (160 km), turning once.

Can't get permission to borrow the car? Cook in a preheated 400°F oven for 15 minutes.

Since the introduction of *Le Guide Michelin*, French chefs have preserved their coveted stars by creating recipes that require tools most lay cooks don't know how to pronounce, let alone find. Cooking *en papillote*, for example, is the classic French technique of baking food between sealed sheets of parchment paper. This method allows fish and meats to steam in their own juices, delivering succulent results without large quantities of butter or oil (that is, unless you eat the oil-soaked paper). In my quest to demystify haute cuisine, I have discovered that almost anything that can be cooked in parchment paper can also be baked to juicy perfection in a standard-issue brown paper lunch bag. Unlike car-engine cooking, this method is as functional as it is fun. Now that the word is out, there is one less obstacle standing between you and your own Michelin star.

the paper work

1   Drizzle a tablespoon of olive oil over the outside of each bag and rub it with your hand until all surfaces of the bag (inside and out) have absorbed the oil. (This is a perfect application for olive oil sprays or misters. If you have one, spray bags generously, then rub oil into paper.)

2   Place ingredients and seasonings inside the bags, force out the excess air, then tightly roll bags shut. Place in the oven on a cookie sheet and bake according to directions.

3   The bag will brown, but it will not burn. As the food cooks and lets off steam, the bag should puff up slightly. When the food is fully cooked, bring the bags to the table on individual plates and let each guest slit them open. If you rip open the bag only to discover that the contents are not fully cooked, the jig is up. Wrap the opened bag in aluminum foil and return it to the oven until fully cooked.

brown-bagged sea bass with papaya salsa

serves 2

I originally concocted this recipe to show off my paper-bag technique. Then a funny thing happened on the way to my testing dinners. It was so much fun to serve, and so well received, that it quickly evolved into one of the bright lights of my repertoire. Its charms are obvious: dead-easy preparation, healthy ingredients, fresh tropical flavors, colorful presentation, and the joy of wowing your guests—all in one simple recipe. Try it—a brilliant dinner is practically in the bag.

brown-bagged sea bass

2	tablespoons olive oil, or a lesser amount of olive oil spray
2	lunch-size brown paper bags
2	(6-ounce) sea bass fillets
1	teaspoon freshly ground black pepper
1	tablespoon soy sauce
1.	tablespoon freshly squeezed lime juice
1 1/2	tablespoons freshly grated ginger, *peeled before grating*

1 Preheat oven to 425°F.
2 Drizzle 1 tablespoon of oil over the outside of each bag and rub it with your hand until all surfaces of the bag have absorbed the oil.
3 Rinse fillets, then pat dry. Pepper both sides.
4 In a small bowl, mix soy sauce, lime juice, and ginger.
5 Set bags on their broad side and place one fillet flat inside each bag. Then, using a tablespoon, reach into the bag and spoon half of the soy-lime-ginger mixture over each of the fillets. Force excess air from the bags, roll up the open ends, and tightly crimp to seal shut.
6 Bake on a cookie sheet for 10 minutes. Remove and serve immediately. Instruct guests to slit open bags, peel back the paper, and spoon Papaya Salsa overtop.

papaya salsa

1	ripe papaya (ripe = slightly soft to the touch), *skinned, seeded, then diced into 1/4-inch cubes. If papayas are unavailable, replace with a mango.*
2	scallions, *trimmed, then diced*
1/4	cup lightly packed cilantro, *chopped, stems removed before measuring*
2	tablespoons freshly squeezed lime juice
2	tablespoons red bell pepper or red cabbage (for color), *finely chopped*
1	jalapeño chili, *seeds and membranes removed, minced*

1 Combine all ingredients in a bowl and toss. Set aside and serve at the table with the sea bass.

music to bag by James Brown. *20 All-Time Greatest Hits.* Yes, Papa's got a brand-new bag.
recommended wine Viognier (pronounced "V-N-A"). This varietal, which tastes like a cross between Chardonnay and Gewürztraminer, is much easier to drink than it is to pronounce. The ripe tropical fruit notes in the wine pair naturally with the ginger and papaya flavors of the fish.

brown-bagged lemon-tarragon chicken with capers

serves 2

Trapping the herbal fragrances in a bag allows the tarragon to permeate—not just decorate.

2	tablespoons of olive oil, or a lesser amount of olive oil spray
2	lunch-size brown paper bags
2	(6-ounce) boneless, skinless chicken breasts, *white tendons removed*
1	teaspoon salt
1	teaspoon freshly ground black pepper
2	tablespoons fresh tarragon, *chopped, stems discarded before measuring*
1	tablespoon capers
1	tablespoon freshly squeezed lemon juice
1	tablespoon white wine (Skip this if you don't have an opened bottle around and add an extra tablespoon of lemon juice instead.)

1 Preheat oven to 425°F.
2 Drizzle 1 tablespoon of olive oil over the outside of each bag and rub it with
your hand until all surfaces of the bag have absorbed the oil.
3 Turn the smooth, shiny side of the breasts up and pound them with a mallet until they
are approximately half of their original thickness. Salt and pepper both sides.
4 Sprinkle tarragon and capers evenly over the chicken.
5 Set bags on their broad side and place one chicken breast flat inside each bag.
Reach in and spoon half of the lemon juice and wine overtop each chicken breast.
Force excess air from the bags, roll up the open ends, and tightly crimp to seal shut.
6 Bake for 15 minutes on a cookie sheet. Remove and serve immediately. Instruct
guests to slit open bags and peel back the paper.

music to bag by Various artists. *Music from the Motion Picture: Jackie Brown.* Sixties and seventies
soul music handpicked by director Quentin Tarantino.
recommended wine A red wine from the Côtes du Rhone or a rosé from the Côtes de Provence area
of France is the typical accompaniment to this (reconfigured) traditional Provençal dish.
specialized cooking apparatus mallet

Cooking with an iron is easier than pressing a shirt. Why bother? Maybe you forgot to pay the gas bill. Or perhaps, like Denzel Washington's character in Spike Lee's flick *He Got Game*, you frequent low-rent flophouses where "room service" charges by the hour—and wants the money up front. At Motel 6 they don't deliver anything. And if you are lucky enough to be holed up in a swish hotel that provides plenty of the old-fashioned kind of room service, you'd better be ready to pay the price. There the average grilled-cheese sandwich can cost upward of fifteen bucks (including tax, service charges, and mandatory tip). Sure the accompanying crisp white linens, fresh-cut flowers, and miniature condiments can dress it up to look like haute cuisine—but at the end of the day, it's still just a grilled-cheese sandwich. The next time the craving strikes, dial housekeeping, not room service. Once you have ironed yourself the classic American snack, you might even be inspired to use the iron for something truly wacky, like getting the wrinkles out of your shirt.

the instruction manual

There are two main styles of iron cooking: The facedown method and the faceup method. A third variation involves resting the iron on the rim of a small bowl and steaming the contents. Despite my success steaming broccoli, I have not expanded upon this technique because of the plethora of safety hazards it creates.

facedown method (see photo A) Assemble your sandwich, quesadilla, or wrap. Insert it in a standard-issue brown paper lunch bag, or wrap it in aluminum foil, and set a preheated iron on top for 3 to 4 minutes per side. If the sandwich has a flat surface, let the full weight of the iron rest on the package. There is no need to hold it in place. For reasons I cannot explain, it is not necessary to use butter to grease the surface of the bag or the foil. Wrapped store-bought foods such as refrigerated burritos can be heated in their original packaging after making a small incision to allow hot air to escape—as long as there is no plastic involved.

faceup method (see photo B) Take an 8 x 10-inch piece of aluminum foil and make a $1/2$-inch fold along each edge of the foil. Fold over three times to build "walls," thereby creating a makeshift pan. Hold the iron upside down, place the foil pan on the hot surface, and use it like a hot plate. If you prop up the iron between two pillows or any other combustible objects, don't even think of mentioning my name at the trial.

music to iron by Whatever is on MTV or VH1.

A

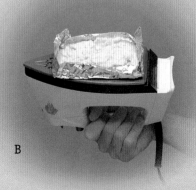

B

your basic pressed-cheese sandwich
serves 1

In your quest to become an iron man or woman, begin with the simplest form of grilled sandwich: the classic American grilled cheese. Once you've mastered the art of pressing cheese between crisply browned slices of Wonder bread, you can expand your horizons to include international specialties. Try a simple quesadilla: Monterey Jack cheese and a few slices of jalapeño chili melted between two small flour tortillas. Then, when you are ready for a greater challenge, take your cue from the Italians, who have turned grilled sandwiches into an art form called *panini*. In addition to a wide variety of cheeses, they add grilled eggplant, roasted bell pepper, and thinly sliced meats.

1	slice of American cheese, or the equivalent amount of any superior foreign import
2	slices of Wonder bread, or any other sliced bread
1	(12 x 12-inch) sheet of aluminum foil, or 1 small brown paper bag

1 Preheat iron on the "linen" setting.
2 Place cheese between the two slices of bread. Either wrap foil around sandwich and pinch to seal or stick sandwich in the bag and roll up the end.
3 Following the facedown method, carefully balance the iron on top of the package for approximately 3 minutes. Flip sandwich and repeat on the other side for another 3 minutes.

pressed eggs–sunny side up, or scrambled
serves 1

For a complete breakfast, iron yourself a piece of toast

1	pat of butter
2	eggs
1	(12 x 10-inch) sheet of aluminum foil
1	drinking glass

1 Preheat iron on the "linen" setting.
2 Make your pan (see Instruction Manual). Rub the inside with butter.
3 Break eggs into drinking glass (for scrambled eggs, use a fork to beat eggs).
4 Following the faceup method, hold iron upright, place aluminum foil over the face. When butter begins to sizzle, use your free hand to pour eggs onto foil. Cook to desired degree of doneness.

dry-clean only

During my experimental mode, I had some initial success making Jiffy Pop popcorn on an upturned iron. Unfortunately, I have been unable to reproduce anything better than half-popped results on a regular basis.

isn't it ironic

A woman was in her kitchen, preparing a pot roast for dinner. As she was cutting the ends off the roast, her husband walked in. This sight piqued his curiosity, and he asked his wife why it was necessary to discard the ends.

"It's the way my mother always does it, and her roasts are always perfect," she responded.

The next time his mother-in-law was visiting, the husband took the opportunity to ask her why she trims the ends off her pot roast.

"It's the way my mother always did it, and she was revered for her roasts," she said.

On a subsequent trip to the grandmother's, the increasingly perplexed man posed the same question to the matriarch of the family. She paused for a moment to recall her glory days of cooking, then answered. "The only reason I ever cut the ends off my roast was that the pot was too small."

It's always impressive to see flames leap out of a pan and lick the ceiling of a restaurant kitchen. But for some reason, most of us are not keen on willfully setting fires on our own stoves. Too bad. The pyrotechnics are not just for show. Burning alcohol intensifies the inherent flavors of whatever is in the pan. Each individual spirit imparts its own characteristics to the food when set alight—which is why some natural pairings have become classics. It's easier than it looks to flambé like a professional chef. Read the following Fire Regulations, then pour 1 to 2 ounces of your chosen hooch into a pan of food, let it heat up for about five seconds, and torch it. The flames should jump about two feet high, then burn out after about ten seconds (along with most of the alcoholic content). There are many traditional flambéed dishes, but none are as simple as dessert. Here are three of my favorites that are more than just a flash in the pan.

fire regulations

clear the decks To keep the flames from burning down the kitchen, clear the area of any flammable objects and move your fire extinguisher within easy reach.

cap it If you have big hair, wear a hat.

reduce it Too much liquid in the pan will dilute the alcohol and prevent it from igniting. Simmer contents until no more than 2 to 3 tablespoons remain before adding alcohol.

keep your distance If you have a gas stove, beware that spattering particles may cause the alcohol to ignite prematurely.

put a lid on it Keep a lid within easy reach. If the flames burn too high, or for more than 10 seconds, cover the pan with a lid.

music to flambé by

The Flaming Lips *Transmissions from the Satellite Heart*. Noise-pop paradise.
The Flamin' Groovies *Teenage Head*. Teen angst from the legendary San Francisco band.
Combustible Edison *I, Swinger*. The first record from the Cocktail Nation's Commanders in Chief.
Talking Heads *Speaking in Tongues*. Featuring "Burning Down the House."
Sylvester *12x12: The Sylvester Collection*. A disco inferno.

ignited apple crisp

serves 4

Spark up the old standard with this short-order version.

4	tablespoons granulated sugar
3	tablespoons butter
4	apples, *peeled, cored, and sliced into* ^{1}/8-inch slices
1	cup premium granola
3	ounces Calvados (a French apple brandy) or applejack (the American version)
1	pint vanilla ice cream or frozen yogurt

1 In a dry sauté pan over medium heat, add sugar. Stir occasionally for 5 minutes, or until sugar has melted and turned into a smooth golden liquid.
2 Remove from heat and stir in butter until it has melted and blended with the sugar.
3 Return pan to heat and add apples to liquid. Stir for 5 minutes, or until they are lightly browned.
4 Add granola and toss for 30 seconds.
5 Pour in Calvados, let it heat up for 10 seconds, then ignite.
6 After flames burn out, serve immediately over individual scoops of ice cream.

le secret Once granola has been added, don't take any time-outs or the granola will lose its crunch.

blazing bananas

serves 4

Use up those browning bananas without the fuss and muss of baking banana bread.

4	tablespoons granulated sugar
3	tablespoons butter
4	bananas, *peeled and sliced as if slicing into a bowl of cereal*
3	ounces dark rum
1	pint vanilla ice cream or frozen yogurt

1 Add sugar to a dry sauté pan over medium heat. Stir occasionally for 5 minutes, or until sugar has melted and turned into a smooth golden liquid.
2 Remove from heat and stir in butter until it has melted and blended with the sugar.
3 Return pan to heat and add bananas to liquid. Stir for 5 minutes, or until they are lightly browned.
4 Pour in rum, let it heat up for 10 seconds, then ignite.
5 After flames burn out, serve immediately over individual scoops of ice cream.

le secret Use ripe (but not overripe and mushy) bananas.

pyrotechnic pineapple

serves 4

The USDA recommends 2 to 4 servings of fresh fruit a day. How you eat it is your business.

1	ripe pineapple
3	tablespoons butter
4	tablespoons granulated sugar
3	ounces Grand Marnier
1	pint vanilla ice cream or frozen yogurt

1 Sit the pineapple on its side, and slice it in half vertically through the leafy section (see illustration). Chisel out the core of each half and discard. Then cut around the fleshy sections with a knife (as you would a grapefruit). Remove flesh with a spoon and cut into small chunks. Set aside both the flesh and the rinds.

2 Melt butter in a sauté pan over medium-high heat. Add pineapple chunks, but none of the juice, and stir occasionally for 5 minutes.

3 Add 1 tablespoon of sugar and stir for 1 minute, or until it has dissolved. Repeat the process, a tablespoon at a time, with the remaining sugar.

4 Pour in Grand Marnier, let it heat up for 10 seconds, then ignite.

5 Place a single scoop of ice cream in each of the hollowed-out pineapple shells and pour half the contents of pan overtop each. Serve immediately with two spoons per couple.

le secret Use a very ripe pineapple. (The smell test is the most reliable way of determining ripeness.)

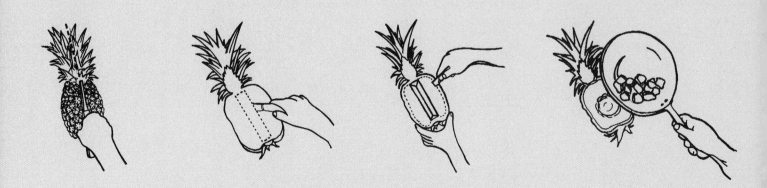

surreal meals

eat your art out

surrealism: sə-'rē-ə-li-zem
natural objects in unnatural juxtapositions

I am frequently asked, "Why are you called The Surreal Gourmet?" The truth is that the moniker was inspired by the garlic-induced illustrations I created to accompany the otherwise very real recipes in my first book. Unfortunately, the truth just isn't good enough for some people. One skeptical Australian reviewer went out of his way to chastise me for not presenting food that lived up to its Surreal billing. My first reaction was to cry foul. After all, does the Galloping Gourmet really gallop? Is the Frugal Gourmet really frugal? But something in the reviewer's criticism lingered in my mind until it provoked an epiphany. From that moment on, I accepted the mission to fully embrace my nom de plume, and I became a fool for faux. Now I amuse myself by concocting cocktail appetizers and multicourse meals that are prepared from one set of ingredients but presented to look like something entirely different. These edible *trompe l'oeils* have proven to be as much fun for the company as they are for the cook. Try one at your next dinner party—chances are your guests will not have had the same thing for lunch.

shrimp "on the bar-b"

As they say in Australia, "Good on ya." See chipotle dry-rub shrimp (page 30).

ham & "eggs"

serves 4 as an appetizer

This visual twist on the classic pairing of melon and prosciutto will provide an *egg*centric beginning to any meal.

2	honeydew melons
1	cantaloupe melon
1/3	pound prosciutto (see page 135)
2	sprigs parsley

1 Cut four 1/4-inch slices from each honeydew melon (see diagram on page 140).
2 Shape honeydew slices to look like the egg white of a sunny-side-up egg.
3 Slice the cantaloupe in half and use a melon scoop or a measuring tablespoon to carve out two "yolks."
4 Trim the melon balls to resemble yolks.
5 Assemble "eggs" and position prosciutto alongside them.
6 Garnish with parsley and serve immediately, or refrigerate.

specialized cooking apparatus melon scoop or measuring tablespoon
props For the best contrast, use solid-color plates that are neither white nor yellow.

"roe" boat

Row your roe boat gently up the champagne stream.

smoked salmon "carrots"

serves 8 as an appetizer

The silly wabbit in everyone will munch up these *dillicious* canapés.

1/2	cup cream cheese, *at room temperature*
1	tablespoon capers, *drained of all brine*
1	lemon, *zested (see page 140), then squeezed*
1/2	teaspoon freshly ground black pepper
1	bunch fresh dill. *Stem and mince 3 tablespoons' worth. Reserve remaining stems for garnish.*
4	slices pumpernickel bread (the dense, thinly sliced type that comes in a block)
8	ounces smoked salmon

1 In a food processor, blend cream cheese, capers, lemon zest, lemon juice, black pepper, and minced dill, until smooth. If you don't have a processor, mince capers by hand, then mash with the other ingredients.
2 Spread a 1/8-inch layer of cream cheese mixture over pumpernickel slices (see diagram page 140).
3 Cover cream cheese mixture with a single layer of salmon. Double up where the salmon gets thin.
4 Use the sharpest knife available to trim all edges, then slice into long triangles and round the top edges.
5 Select the best-looking dill sprigs and bare the stems after an inch of dill top. Place canapés on a serving plate, then insert a 1-inch dill sprig "carrot top" in each canapé between the salmon and the bread.

le secret Use the best smoked salmon available (or affordable).
specialized cooking apparatus food processor
props gardening gloves for the server

"ground" olives

See citrus tapenade (page 40).

"palate" pleasing dips

Mix and match your own dips and spreads with store-bought favorites.

fromage fatale

A killer cheese tray.

bucket of shells

Use your favorite paella or seafood recipe or see "not luck" bouillabaisse (page 116).

"diced" fish

serves 4 as an entrée

Life is a crapshoot. But the odds are good that your lucky guests will be impressed by this fish dish.

fish

1	(20-ounce) fillet of a firm-fleshed fish (e.g., shark), cut 1¹/4 inch thick
1	teaspoon olive oil
2	tablespoons freshly squeezed lime juice
	salt and freshly ground pepper to taste
1	tablespoon whole black peppercorns

cilantro sauce

See Piquant Dill Sauce (page 56). Prepare according to directions, but replace dill with fresh cilantro, and replace lemon juice with lime juice.

1 Make cilantro sauce or your own favorite sauce. Reheat before serving.
2 Preheat oven to 400°F.
3 With a very sharp knife, cut fish into eight 1¹/4-inch cubes (see diagrams on page 140). Use scraps for fishwiches, or cat food.
4 Rub oil over two 12 x 16-inch sheets of aluminum foil. Turn up the edges.
5 Place half the cubes in the center of each piece of foil. Drizzle with lime juice. Add salt and pepper.
6 Seal packages (see page 140) and bake for 10 minutes.
7 Remove from foil and use the tip of a paring knife to make small holes for the peppercorns. Gently press peppercorns into holes.
8 Spoon sauce onto warmed plates. Top with two "dice" and serve immediately.

"bed" of polenta

serves 2 as an entrée

A couple of years ago I appeared on a midafternoon talk show alongside *Playboy*'s Miss April '96. I created this polenta bed with ravioli pillows in her honor. You can make the Roasted Red Bell Pepper Sauce from scratch (see page 138) or save time by using any store-bought red sauce or pesto.

polenta "bed"

   1   cup polenta

1 Prepare polenta according to package directions (for additional flavor, replace water with chicken stock, and add salt and pepper, chopped fresh herbs, and freshly grated Parmigiano-Reggiano cheese).
2 Spread a $^3/4$-inch layer of cooked polenta in a greased 8 x 10-inch baking pan and let set until solid (this may take an hour or so).
3 Cut two 4 x 5-inch slabs of polenta.
4 Just before serving, finish polenta by sautéing in a pan with one or two teaspoons of olive oil for approximately 5 minutes per side, or until it is browned and crispy on the outside.

pasta "sheet"

   2   sheets fresh uncut pasta, *cut into 5-inch squares*. (You can find uncut sheets of pasta at fresh pasta stores. Alternatively, use extra wide sheets of dried lasagna pasta and make single "beds.")

1 Boil pasta in a large pot according to package directions.
2 Strain pasta into a colander that has been coated with olive oil on the inside (to avoid stickage).

ravioli "pillows"

   4   pieces fresh ravioli

1 Boil ravioli according to directions.
2 Strain ravioli into a colander that has been coated with olive oil on the inside.

Assemble beds on warmed plates, then spoon sauce around perimeter.

specialty ingredient
whole pasta sheets

iced "coffee"

serves 4 as a dessert

A perfect first canvas for budding Surrealists.

1	pint coffee ice cream or frozen yogurt
8	cookies of your choice

1 Remove ice cream from freezer and let stand for 10 minutes, or until malleable. Scoop into coffee cups or mugs and use the back of a spoon to create a smooth surface $^1/4$ inch below the rim of the cup. Return to freezer and let harden.

2 Place cups on saucers, garnish with cookies and serve.

props coffee cups and saucers, or mugs

pound cake "fries" with raspberry "catsup"

serves 2 as a dessert, with leftover sauce for your next dish of ice cream

Have them my way.

pound cake "fries"

1/4	loaf of pound cake, *cut into 1/4-inch slices*
1	cardboard French fry container (ask politely and you shall receive)

1 Cut pound cake slices into 1/4-inch strips.
2 Arrange strips on a toaster oven rack and toast until browned on top and bottom. Turn strips and toast until remaining two sides are browned. Let cool, then arrange in container.

raspberry "catsup"

1	12-ounce bag frozen raspberries, *thawed*, or 2 cups fresh raspberries
2	tablespoons confectionery (icing) sugar
1	empty catsup squeeze bottle

1 Place raspberries in a blender or food processor, and puree (add 1 or 2 tablespoons of water or lemon juice, if necessary, to facilitate blending).
2 Add sugar, one teaspoon at a time, to taste, until tartness is gone.
3 Place raspberry puree in a fine mesh strainer over a bowl. Use a rubber spatula to force the puree through the strainer. Discard the seeds, and transfer the puree to the squeeze bottle. Serve alongside "fries."

specialized cooking apparatus toaster oven
props French fry container; squeeze bottle

cinematic suppers

five dinner-and-a-video double features

There is no torture worse than choking on stale popcorn in a cramped theater while watching sumptuous meals being prepared on-screen in mouthwatering detail. Even Dolby Surround Sound can't drown out the growling noise of a jealous stomach. Now that the lag time from the big screen to Blockbuster is shorter than a Hollywood romance, why not stay home—where you can have your film and eat it, too? To help motivate you, I have picked five of my favorite food-related movies and paired them with dishes that they have featured or inspired. Each double bill is guaranteed to make you salivate, then satisfy your cravings. I've also included thematically related cocktails and spiced popcorn recipes for those who would prefer to stay close to the couch. These cinematic suppers are life imitating art at its most delicious.

big night

"To have the knowledge of God is the bread of angels."
—Primo

★★★★★

Primo, a passionate chef, and Secondo, his business-minded brother, immigrate to the land of opportunity, circa 1950, and attempt to introduce authentic Italian cuisine to the uninitiated on the Jersey shore. Across the street, a schmaltzy Italian restaurant thrives by giving the people what they want—namely, spaghetti and meatballs. The constant struggle of art versus commerce pits the brothers against each other as they strive to make their restaurant survive. Mix in some inspired Old World cooking, a few romantic interests, and the legendary big-band leader Louis Prima, and the pasta pot boileth over.

seafood risotto

serves 2

This dish is the star of the most antagonistic food sequence since Jack Nicholson ordered toast in *Five Easy Pieces*. Even though the scallops and shrimp were not visible to the chain-smoking "philistine" who ordered this on-screen, you will taste them in every bite.

2	tablespoons olive oil
3	garlic cloves, *minced*
1	leek, white and pale green section only, *finely chopped, then washed thoroughly*
4	cups fish stock, if available, or chicken or vegetable stock
1	cup arborio rice (Available in many grocery stores and all Italian food stores.)
1/2	cup white wine
1/4	pound uncooked shrimp, *shelled and deveined (see page 140), chopped coarsely*
1/4	pound scallops, *chopped into small pieces* (Buy the less expensive small scallops.)
1/4	cup Italian parsley, *stems discarded before measuring, finely chopped*
1 1/2	tablespoons fresh tarragon, *minced, stems discarded before measuring*
1	tablespoon butter, *at room temperature*
1/2	tablespoon freshly ground black pepper
1/2	cup Parmigiano-Reggiano (see page 135), *freshly grated*. (Note: Primo would disapprove of the untraditional combination of parmesan with seafood risotto, but Secondo would applaud it.)

1 In a heavy medium-size pot over medium-high heat, add olive oil. Immediately add garlic and leek, and stir for 4 minutes, or until the leek is translucent.
2 In a second pot, bring stock to a boil, then reduce heat and allow to simmer.
3 Add rice to the garlic and leeks, and stir vigorously until all the rice grains are coated in oil.
4 Add wine to rice, reduce heat to medium, and stir for 2 minutes, or until most of the liquid is absorbed.
5 Use a ladle to add half a cup of the hot stock to the rice. Stir frequently. Each time the stock is

almost fully absorbed, add another half cup. After 15 minutes, add the shrimp and scallops. Continue stirring and adding stock until rice is creamy yet still a little firm to the bite. (It may not be necessary to use all of the stock.) From this point it should take approximately 5 more minutes for the last touch of stock to be absorbed. The total cooking time, once the rice has been added, should not be more than about 25 minutes.

6   Remove from the heat. Stir in parsley, tarragon, butter, pepper, and three quarters of the parmesan. Serve on warmed plates and top with a sprinkle of parmesan.

le secret To keep the rice slightly creamy, don't wait until the last ladleful of stock is totally absorbed before serving.

suggested accompaniment Baby green salad with a vinaigrette (see page 138), and crusty bread.

the adventure club Replace the shrimp and scallops with an equal amount of lobster meat.

music to cook by Various artists. *Big Night: Original Motion Picture Soundtrack*. The second track alone on this great collection is worth the price of the disc.

recommended wine Orvieto. The crisp acidity and aromatic nose make this a good foil for dominant seafood flavors.

negroni
serves 2

Possibly an acquired taste—but well worth the pursuit.

1	ounce Campari
1	ounce sweet vermouth
1	ounce gin
4	ounces soda water

1   Pour one half Campari, vermouth, and gin into each of two rocks glasses or wine glasses, over ice. Stir and top with a splash of soda. Garnish with an orange twist.

parmigiano popcorn
makes 8 cups

2	tablespoons vegetable oil
1/2	cup popcorn kernels
1	teaspoon fennel seeds (optional), *chopped finely*
1/4	cup freshly grated Parmigiano-Reggiano cheese (see page 135)
1/2	teaspoon salt
1/2	teaspoon freshly ground black pepper

1   In a medium-size pot over high heat add oil and one kernel of popcorn. Cook until kernel pops.

2   Add the rest of the popcorn to the oil and cover with a lid.

3   When corn starts popping, open lid, toss in fennel, and re-cover.

4   Shake pot constantly until popping stops.

5   Empty popcorn into a bowl and sprinkle with parmesan, salt, and pepper. Toss and serve.

who is killing the great chefs of europe

"My body is a work of art created by the finest chefs in the world. Every fold is a brush stroke, every crease a sonnet, every chin a concerto."
—Maximillian Vanderveere

★★★★★

This farcical whodunit follows the woes of Maximillian Vanderveere, the publisher of an epicurean magazine whose stature is matched only by the size of his insatiable appetite. For Max, life is not worth living if he can't have his foie gras and Sauternes (and that's just for breakfast). While the hapless gourmand wrestles with his doctor's orders to halve his girth, an unknown assassin systematically offs several of his favorite chefs, doing them in, in the style of their culinary specialty. Add a three-star food fight, a long tall Texan, and a surprise ending to the mix, and watch Max bite it.

pan-seared duck breast with cassis compote
serves 2

You don't have to be one of the great chefs of Europe to master this *plat du canard*. In fact, before developing this recipe, it had never occurred to me to make duck at home. But this simple French-inspired dish is such a change from the ordinary that now I am hooked. After you have served it in the glow of the tube, try it by candlelight.

2	(6-ounce) boneless duck breasts (They may come as one butterflied breast. If so, slice down the middle to separate them. The best ducks are Moscovy ducks, available from specialty butchers, but any duck will fit the bill.)
1/2	teaspoon salt
1 1/2	teaspoons coarsely ground black pepper
2	shallots, *diced finely*
2	tablespoons crème de cassis (This is a French liqueur made from black currants. Despite the name, it is a syrupy, crimson-colored liqueur.)
4	tablespoons black currant jam (ideally unsweetened), black cherry, or similar preserve
2	tablespoons balsamic vinegar, or red wine vinegar if you have no balsamic on hand

1. Preheat oven to 350°F.
2. Using a sharp knife, score four 1/4-inch-deep cuts across the duck skin at a 45-degree angle *(see diagram A.)* Sprinkle 1/4 teaspoon salt and pepper over the meat side of each duck breast.
3. Heat a sauté pan over high heat. When pan is hot, add duck breasts, skin side down, and cook for 4 minutes, or until skin is brown and crispy. Flip and cook for 2 more minutes.
4. Remove pan from heat (save the drippings) and transfer duck breasts, skin side up, to a cooking sheet lined with aluminum foil. Bake on the top rack of the oven for 6 minutes.
5. Discard all but two tablespoons of duck drippings from the pan. Return pan to medium heat and add shallots. Stir occasionally for 3 minutes, or until shallots begin to turn golden. Add cassis and stir with a wooden spoon to loosen the browned bits left by the duck. Add jam, vinegar, and remaining teaspoon of black pepper, and stir occasionally for 3 minutes. Remove from heat.

6 Remove duck from the oven and slice each breast at a 45-degree angle into 1/4-inch-thick strips (properly cooked duck should resemble medium-rare steak). Arrange in a fanlike pattern on a warmed plate and spoon cassis compote overtop (see diagram B). Serve immediately.

le secret If you are unfamiliar with duck breasts, don't be put off by their unusual look. The fat-to-meat proportions reverse themselves. As it cooks the fat is rendered and the meat expands.

the adventure club Replace jam with an equal amount of fresh black currants, blackberries, or cherries. (Chop fruit coarsely and pit if necessary before adding to pan.) Cook for 6 minutes instead of the 3 minutes indicated at the end of step 5.

suggested accompaniment If the typical French overcooked green beans don't light your fire, serve with sautéed Swiss chard and baked baby potatoes.

music to cook by Serge Gainsbourg. *Comic Strip*. The once-banned, now-revered (but still dead) French provocateur at his pop peak.

recommended wine Côte de Nuits (a red Burgundy) or a Santa Barbara or Oregon pinot noir. Any of these wines should provide a supple, jammy quality that should waddle well with the sauce.

kir royale
serves 2

If you get no kick from Champagne, try it this way with a splash of cassis.

3	tablespoons crème de cassis
12	ounces Champagne

1 Pour half the cassis into each of two flute glasses, then add Champagne.

provençal popcorn
makes 8 cups

1 1/2	tablespoons butter
2	tablespoons vegetable oil
1/2	cup popcorn kernels
1	tablespoon herbes de Provence (available in the spice section of most grocery stores)
1/2	teaspoon salt (If your butter is salted, use a bit less.)

1 Warm butter in a saucepan over medium heat until it melts. Turn off heat and reserve in the pan.
2 In a medium-size pot over high heat, add oil and one kernel of popcorn. Cook until kernel pops.
3 Add the rest of the popcorn to the oil and cover with a lid.
4 When corn starts popping, open lid, toss in herbs, and re-cover.
5 Shake pot constantly until popping stops.
6 Empty popcorn into a bowl, sprinkle with salt, and drizzle butter overtop. Toss and serve.

eat drink man woman

"Without any taste buds of my own anymore, I judge my food by your face."
—Master Chef Chu

★★★★★

An aging Chinese master chef grapples with losing his delicate sense of taste. Meanwhile, his three adult daughters struggle with their own family baggage in the face of their sordid and assorted personal relationships. Set in contemporary Taipei, the film follows each character as they fumble for solutions to their dilemmas. But to hell with the plot; the real story takes place in the kitchen. It's here that the father lovingly assembles the weekly Sunday dinner—a ritual that becomes the backdrop for the family's pivotal revelations. From chasing down a chicken in the back garden to presenting it on the dinner table, the preparation of these elaborate feasts unfolds like the Peking Opera.

happy lobster won tons & lucky stir-fried snow peas
serves 2 as dinner, or 4–6 as an appetizer

These magical little packets explode in your mouth with multilayered flavors and textures. Once you've enjoyed them with the video, mark the page and make them as appetizers for your next cocktail party.

happy lobster won tons

1	tablespoon toasted sesame oil
1	shallot, *diced finely*
6	ounces fresh or thawed lobster tail, *diced*
1	tablespoon freshly grated ginger, *peeled before grating*
3	tablespoons finely grated carrot, *peeled before grating*
$1/4$	cup canned water chestnuts, *drained and diced*
$1/4$	cup canned bamboo shoots, *drained and diced*
$1/2$	teaspoon hot chili oil (a.k.a. Mongolian fire oil), or to taste
2	scallions, *diced finely*
5	tablespoons soy sauce
1	tablespoon powdered wasabi, or English mustard powder
1	package $3^1/2$-inch square won ton wrappers (available in the refrigerated section of most grocery stores)
$1/4$	cup cornstarch
2	cups peanut or canola oil, for frying

1 In a sauté pan over medium-high heat, add sesame oil.
2 Add shallot and sauté until it shows the first sign of turning golden.
3 Add lobster, ginger, carrot, chestnuts, bamboo, green onions, and chili oil. Stir for 3 minutes, or until lobster is fully cooked. Stir in 1 tablespoon soy sauce. Remove from heat and let cool.

4   While the lobster mixture is cooling, make dipping sauce by placing wasabi in a small bowl. Slowly blend in approximately two teaspoons water, until you have a smooth paste the consistency of prepared mustard. Then slowly blend in 4 tablespoons of soy sauce. Set aside.

5   Place a small bowl of warm water beside won ton skins. Line a cookie sheet with waxed paper and dust lightly with cornstarch. Place it within easy reach. Put a single won ton skin in the palm of your hand and spoon 1 teaspoon of lobster mixture into the center. DO NOT OVERSTUFF. Wrap (see *diagrams.*) Before each fold, dip fingers in the water (think of it as glue) and dampen the skin at the points at which the next flap will be folded. Make sure flaps overlap generously and all seams are securely "glued." If any tears appear in the wrapper, dump out the contents and start over. Set the finished won tons on the tray. Do not let them touch one another. If you are not frying won tons immediately, cover with a damp dish towel and refrigerate.

6   Pour canola oil into a heavy skillet until it is $1/2$ inch deep. Turn heat to medium-high and heat oil. When you think oil is ready, drop in a tiny piece of a won ton skin. If oil sizzles immediately, you are ready to rock. If oil begins to smoke at any time, remove pan from the heat and allow to cool slightly. Fry as many won tons at one time as your skillet will accommodate—without letting them touch. Fry for 30 seconds, or until the bottom side is golden brown. Then turn over for 15 more seconds, or until second side is the same color. Remove with a slotted spoon and transfer onto paper towels or a large brown paper grocery bag to drain excess oil. Proceed to next batch. Serve immediately with dipping sauce.

le secret Use only fresh won ton skins. Poorly stored skins will crack when folded. And be sure to sprinkle the cornstarch generously to keep won tons from sticking.

variations on a theme For shrimp, chicken, or tofu won tons, replace lobster with an equal amount of diced shrimp, ground chicken, or well-drained firm tofu. (The sautéing time for the chicken will be about double.) For extra flavor, add a palmful of chopped fresh mint leaves.

note Wrapping won tons is labor-intensive. However, once you get rolling, you will pick up speed.

tips for advance prep Won tons can be made up to a day in advance and refrigerated or frozen. To freeze won tons, dust them with cornstarch and set between layers of waxed paper. Avoid letting them touch. To use, let thaw for 30 minutes, then follow frying instructions.

specialized cooking apparatus manual dexterity

specialty ingredients won ton skins

music to wrap by Fantastic Plastic Machine. *The Fantastic Plastic Machine.* DJ extraordinaire Tomoyuki Tanaka revisits the '60s.

recommended wine Puligny-Montrachet. This white Burgundy, made from the chardonnay grape, has sweet, floral notes, with less oakiness than you get from most California chards.

(continued on next page)

lucky stir-fried snow peas

This simple accompaniment will transform the won tons into a full meal.

1¹/₂	teaspoons peanut or toasted sesame oil
1	teaspoon freshly grated ginger, *peeled first*
1	garlic clove, *minced*
¹/₃	pound snow peas, *trimmed*
¹/₄	teaspoon soy sauce

1 In a wok or sauté pan over high heat, add oil. When oil is hot, add garlic and ginger and stir for 30 seconds.
2 Add snow peas and stir constantly for 2 minutes, or until they are fully cooked but still crisp. Add soy sauce, toss quickly, then serve alongside won tons.

suggested running order Make the snow peas while the won ton oil is heating up.

chinese beer
serves 2

The Chinese culture may not be known for its cocktails, but it can be credited with this fine beer.

2	bottles Tsingtao beer

1 Open bottles. Pour into glasses.

five-spice popcorn
makes 8 cups

2	tablespoons vegetable oil
¹/₂	cup popcorn kernels
2	teaspoons five-spice powder (Available in the spice or Asian section of your grocery store.)
1	teaspoon soy sauce
1	tablespoon toasted sesame oil

1 In a medium-size pot over high heat, add oil and one kernel of popcorn. Cook until kernel pops.
2 Add the rest of the popcorn to the oil and cover with a lid.
3 When corn starts popping, open lid, toss in five-spice powder, and re-cover.
4 Shake pot constantly until popping stops.
5 Empty popcorn into a bowl, and drizzle with sesame oil and soy sauce. Toss and serve.

building a better chopstick

attack of the killer tomatoes

"All we wanted was a bigger, healthier tomato."
—Government official

★★★★★

It doesn't get any better (or worse, depending on your point of view) than this campy, ultra-low-budget cult classic. The 1977 film is based on the simple what-if premise that if birds, rats, and gorillas can terrorize the world, why can't tomatoes? Along the way, it mocks many of the TV shows and movies of its day. With such a complex plot device, there is no need for big-time actors or special effects—and believe me, you don't get any. Be sure to have a Very Bloody Mary (or two) before you hit "play."

killer gazpacho
serves 2, with leftovers for the next day

Made from a cornucopia of fresh garden vegetables, this traditional chilled Spanish soup is truly to die for.

1	pound ripe tomatoes
2	scallions
1	red bell pepper, *seeds removed*
1	celery stalk
1–2	garlic cloves, *minced*
2/3	cup lightly packed cilantro, *stems discarded before measuring*
1–2	jalapeño chilies, *seeds removed*
1/2	cucumber, *skinned*
2	tablespoons olive oil
1 1/2	tablespoons balsamic or red wine vinegar
2	tablespoons freshly squeezed lemon juice
1/2	teaspoon salt
1	teaspoon freshly ground black pepper
1	cup canned tomato juice

1 Core the stems from the tomatoes, then cut a small "**X**" at the bottom of each. Drop tomatoes into a pot of boiling water for 15 seconds. Remove, let cool for a minute, then peel off the skins. Dice the tomatoes.
2 Chop remaining veggies, then toss in a large bowl along with oil, vinegar, lemon juice, salt, and pepper.
3 Transfer small batches to a blender or food processor and pulse until mixture is a coarse liquid. Thin with tomato juice. Chill in refrigerator for 2 hours, then serve.

le secret Attempt gazpacho with in-season tomatoes only, not the plastic variety.
the adventure club Make your own croutons (see page 139) and sprinkle over soup.

specialized cooking apparatus blender or food processor
suggested accompaniment garlic bread
music to cook by Bob Dylan. *Blood on the Tracks*. One of Dylan's classics.
recommended wine Cava. This Spanish sparkling wine is somewhat acidic, which is necessary to stand up to the tomatofest going on in the soup.

very bloody mary

serves 2

One cult classic deserves another.

12	ounces canned tomato juice
2	tablespoons freshly squeezed lemon juice
1	teaspoon Worcestershire sauce
$1/2$	teaspoon Tabasco sauce
$1/4$	teaspoon salt (use celery salt, if available)
$1/4$	teaspoon freshly ground black pepper
$1/2$	teaspoon horseradish (optional)
3	ounces vodka
2	leafy celery stalks (optional)

1 If you have celery salt, use it to coat the rim of the glasses.*
2 Mix all ingredients in a pitcher and pour into tall glasses over ice. Garnish with a celery stalk.

sun-dried-tomato popcorn

makes 8 cups

2	tablespoons vegetable oil
$1/2$	cup popcorn kernels
$1/2$	teaspoon salt
$1/2$	teaspoon freshly ground black pepper
$1^1/2$	tablespoons oil drained from a jar of oil-packed sun-dried tomatoes

1 In a medium-size pot over high heat, add oil and one kernel of popcorn. Cook until kernel pops.
2 Add the rest of the popcorn to the oil and cover with a lid.
3 Shake pot constantly until popping stops.
4 Empty popcorn into a bowl and sprinkle with salt and pepper. Drizzle with sun-dried-tomato oil. Toss and serve.

*To salt the rim: Place a thin layer of celery salt in a small dish or shallow bowl. Take empty glass and moisten its rim with a lemon wedge. Then dip rim in celery salt to coat. Shake off excess.

like water for chocolate

"A breast untouched by love's fire isn't a breast but a ball of dough."
—Narrator

★★★★★

Tita, the youngest daughter of a Mexican ranching family, is prematurely birthed on the kitchen table amid simmering soups, garlic, and cilantro. With that unusual entrance, Tita stakes her claim to the kitchen, where she presides while developing her mystical culinary powers. After blossoming into a sensuous woman, she is forbidden by her bitter mother to marry the man who steals her heart. Instead, she must adhere to the ancient tradition of caring for the old witch. Cooking from the heart, Tita influences the fate of the family tree by conjuring up recipes that arouse, punish, and even kill. As you watch this tale of unrequited love, don't let saltwater tears fall into your chocolate martini.

turkey escalopes with mole
serves 2

Mole is a traditional Mexican sauce that uses a small amount of chocolate to deepen the flavor of its savory ingredients. You won't have to spend two days laboring over it as Tita did, but try to think positive thoughts during the short time it simmers.

turkey escalopes

Turkey escalopes (a.k.a. scallops) are made from slices of uncooked turkey breast that are cut crosswise against the grain. They are available in most grocery stores. Once pounded into thin cutlets, they cook almost instantly in a sauté pan. Make the mole ahead of time, then prepare the escalopes just before serving.

1/2	pound raw turkey breast, *cut into 1/4-inch slices*
1	tablespoon butter
1/2	teaspoon salt
1/2	teaspoon freshly ground pepper

1 Pound turkey breasts with a meat tenderizer until they are half their original thickness. Sprinkle with salt and pepper.
2 Melt butter in a sauté pan over medium-high heat, and cook turkey for approximately 1 minute per side, or until no pink remains. Serve immediately with mole.

mole

makes about 2 cups

Since mole is a bit labor-intensive, there is no sense in making just two servings. The following recipe will make approximately 8 servings of mole sauce. The extra portions will last in the refrigerator for five days or in the freezer for three months. Serve the leftovers over simply prepared poultry, pork, or fish.

2	cups of mixed dried chilies (i.e., mulato, pasilla, ancho, or whatever large whole dried chilies are available in your grocery store), *stems and seeds discarded, broken into small pieces*
2	tablespoons olive oil
1	medium onion, *diced*
1/2	cup skinned peanuts
1/4	cup sesame seeds
1	garlic clove, *minced*
1	(6-inch) corn tortilla, *sliced into thin strips*
1/4	teaspoon cinnamon powder
1/4	teaspoon ground cloves
1/4	teaspoon freshly ground black pepper
2	tablespoons raisins
2	medium tomatoes, *diced*
1 1/4	cups (that's 1 regular-size can) chicken stock
1	ounce dark chocolate, *chopped*

1 Toast chilies in a dry skillet over medium heat for 4 minutes, stirring occasionally, to unlock their flavors. Add 2 1/2 cups of water, bring to a boil, then reduce heat to a simmering level and cover for 5 minutes. Remove from heat, uncover, and allow to cool.

2 In a large sauté pan over medium-high heat, add olive oil and sauté onions and peanuts for 5 minutes, or until the onions become translucent. Add the sesame seeds, garlic, and tortilla strips and sauté for 3 more minutes, or until everything begins to brown. Add cinnamon, clove, pepper, raisins, and tomatoes, reduce heat to medium, and sauté for 4 more minutes. Remove from heat and allow to cool.

3 Place chilies and their liquid in a blender, and puree until smooth. Rinse the skillet they were originally cooked in, then return pureed chili mixture to it and simmer over medium heat for 10 minutes, stirring occasionally.

4 Place all the contents from the second pan in the blender along with the stock, and puree. Stir the pureed mixture into the simmering chili mixture. Add chocolate and simmer the whole lot for another 10 minutes, or until sauce thickens (i.e., thickly coats the back of a wooden spoon). Remove from heat and allow to cool.

5 Place your finest-mesh strainer over a large bowl, pour mole into strainer, and force the mole through it using a rubber spatula. Discard the solids that remain trapped in the strainer.

To serve, reheat mole and spoon 2 to 4 tablespoons over each serving of turkey escalopes.

(continued on next page)

le secret Finished mole should be the consistency of a thick pureed soup. If it is too thin after straining, simmer it in a saucepan until it reaches the desired degree of thickness. If it is too thick, thin it with a small amount of chicken stock.

specialized cooking apparatus blender; strainer

suggested accompaniment Roasted yams and sautéed greens

music to cook by Anything by the inveterate Mexican band Trio Los Panchos. *Más mariachi!*

recommended wine Banyuls (a French red). This combination of late-harvest grapes creates a wine with a bit of residual sugar that is a match made in heaven for the spices and the chocolate. A Châteauneuf-du-Pape or a California Cabernet (neither of which has anything in common with Banyuls) would be my second choice.

chocolate martini
serves 2

The deceptively clear color of this cocktail makes the first sip a truly Surreal experience.

3	ounces vodka
$1^{1}/2$	ounces clear crème de cacao
$^{1}/2$	teaspoon Cointreau, or triple sec (Skip it if you don't have any on hand.)
2	cups ice
2	Hershey's Kisses or Rolo segments

1 Fill a martini shaker or a large glass with ice. Add all ingredients except the candy garnish, and shake or stir. Strain into chilled martini glasses.
2 Garnish with an unwrapped Hershey's Kiss or a single Rolo (or any small chocolate candy).

cumin popcorn
makes 8 cups

1	teaspoon ground cumin
$^{1}/8$	teaspoon cayenne (optional)
$^{1}/2$	teaspoon freshly ground black pepper
2	tablespoons vegetable oil
$^{1}/2$	cup popcorn kernels
$^{1}/2$	teaspoon salt

1 In a small bowl, mix cumin, cayenne, and pepper.
2 In a medium-size pot over high heat, add oil and one kernel of popcorn. Cook until kernel pops.
3 Add the rest of the popcorn to the oil and cover with a lid.
4 When corn starts popping, open lid, toss in spices, and re-cover.
5 Shake pot constantly until popping stops.
6 Empty popcorn into a bowl and sprinkle with salt. Toss and serve.

And the other nominees are...

Film

Tampopo
Babette's Feast
The Cook, the Thief, His Wife & Her Lover
A Chef in Love
La Grande Bouffe
Diner
Alice's Restaurant
Willy Wonka and the Chocolate Factory
The Last Supper (1976)
Fried Green Tomatoes
My Dinner with André
When Harry Met Sally
Five Easy Pieces
Eating Raoul
Goodfellas
Bread and Chocolate
Bananas
The Scent of Green Papaya
Cocktail
One from the Heart
Leaving Las Vegas

Suggested Accompaniment

Instant Japanese noodles
Quail
Sausage
Wild boar
Roast beef
Cheeseburgers
Anything you want (except Alice)
Chocolate fondue
Bread and wine
Duh
Fish paté
Turkey sandwich and salad (dressing on the side)
Chicken sandwich, hold the chicken, hold the mayo
Steak tartare
Spaghetti with tomato sauce
Nutella sandwich
Banana bread
Papaya smoothy
Mixed drinks
Vodka martinis
Maalox

NOT LUCK DINNER PARTIES

five dinner parties to help you get a lot out of life—
regardless of what your lot in life is

Sometimes it's the people with the least money who seem to get the most out of life. My friend Heidi Von Palleske is an actress who constantly teeters on the precipice of the edge. Despite some very successful films, and a few windfalls, her income has never caught up with her talents. Heidi coined the phrase "unmonied elite" to describe herself and the rest of the unapologetic underclass who never have more than a few dollars in their bank accounts but somehow manifest an enviable lifestyle—albeit hand-to-mouth. The unmonied elite don't let a bourgeois obstacle like money interfere with their ability to indulge in life's great pleasures—nor should you. When the mood strikes to throw a dinner party before the check arrives in the mail, all it takes is twenty dollars in seed money and a few pantry staples to throw a "not luck" dinner—a pot luck minus the luck. If low cash flow is the mother of invention, then these low-budget, high-fun dinner parties are her progeny.

The premise is simple: Instead of asking guests to bring prepared dishes, assign each of them one or more specific gourmet ingredients—taking into account the individuals' resourcefulness, finances, proximity to the stores, and punctuality to determine who brings what. I created all of the following menus to rely on the ingredients, not the cook, to do the hard work. Each serves seven guests plus the host. After all the components have arrived, it's a quick and (relatively) simple matter of enlisting a couple of sous-chefs and connecting the dots. The whole meal should take less than 30 minutes to assemble, from start to finish.

At a "Not Luck" Dinner Party, nobody's feelings are hurt when their tuna casserole goes untouched—and best of all, there's no tuna casserole.

the party platform

The twenty dollars of seed money should cover the basic ingredients to be provided by the host. The exception here is the bouillabaisse dinner, which may run a little over budget, depending on how well your pantry is stocked. Almost all guest ingredients cost less than ten dollars.

It is important that every guest brings a component of the meal so that they feel they have a stake in the successful outcome of the evening. If you already have some of the ingredients I have designated as Guest Assignments, exchange them for something from the Host Requirements list, or substitute with flowers, music, or party favors.

Be sure to inform guests that their ingredient is but one piece of a complex jigsaw puzzle. Describe in detail the specific method of torture that will greet anyone who is late and allude to the mysterious curse of the root canal that has haunted previous last-minute cancellations and no-shows. To play it safe, invite the person who is bringing the appetizer components half an hour early.

To avoid Murphy's Law, be very, very specific when assigning guests their ingredient and politely suggest that they don't wait until the last minute to go shopping. That said, part of the fun of a "not luck" dinner is going with the flow and making do with whatever the guests arrive with. ("They didn't have corn oil so I bought corn syrup.")

In addition to their designated ingredient(s), each guest should be asked to bring a bottle of wine or their favorite nonalcoholic beverage.

If you are a social butterfly of the culinarily challenged breed, lure a kitchen-friendly friend to do the cooking by absolving them of their obligation to bring anything. In this case, you must assume responsibility for the unassigned ingredient(s).

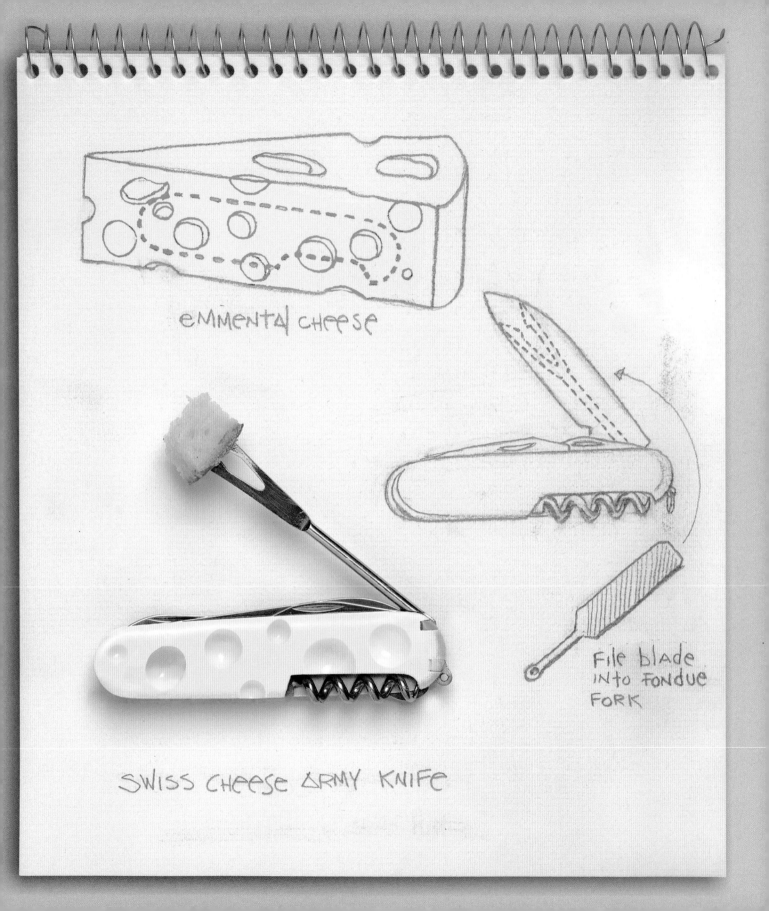

EMMENTAl CHEESE

SWISS CHEESE ARMY KNIFE

File blade
INTO FONDUE
FORK

hot luck fondue party

★ **crudités with balsamic dip** ★ **cheese fondue** ★ **swiss chocolate** ★

a dinner for 8

Rubbing shoulders around the molten cheese and fishing out wayward chunks of crusty bread make fondue parties a natural mixer. What were our parents thinking when they sold the fondue set for fifty cents at their garage sale?

crudités with balsamic dip

Let the guest who brought the veggies wash and trim them while you blend the dip.

crudités

4	carrots, *peeled and sliced*
3	heads Belgian endives, *separated*
1	red pepper, *membranes and seeds removed, sliced into $1/4$-inch strips*
1	head broccoli, *separated into bite-size florets*

balsamic dip

$1/4$	cup balsamic vinegar
$1/4$	cup olive oil
2	tablespoons Dijon mustard
2	tablespoons freshly squeezed lemon juice
$1/4$	teaspoon salt
$1/4$	teaspoon freshly ground black pepper
1	tablespoon honey
1	small shallot, *minced*

1 Puree all ingredients in a blender for 30 seconds. Serve in a bowl alongside veggies.

cheese fondue

According to Swiss tradition, anyone who loses a piece of bread in the cheese must go around the table and kiss each member of the opposite sex.

1	pound Emmental (Swiss cheese), *coarsely grated* (If you do not have a grater, the cheese can be sliced into thin strips.)
1	pound Gruyère, *coarsely grated*
$1/4$	cup flour
$1/4$	teaspoon ground nutmeg
$1/2$	teaspoon freshly ground black pepper
3	cups any dry white wine
1	garlic clove, *cut in half*
2	ounces kirsch (cherry brandy)
2	loaves fresh crusty French, Italian, or sourdough bread, *cut into bite-size chunks with one edge of crust on each bite*

1. Place cheese in a large bowl. Sprinkle flour, nutmeg, and pepper overtop, then toss thoroughly so that the flour evenly coats the cheese.
2. Heat wine in a medium-size pot, over medium-high heat, until tiny bubbles begin to rise to the surface.
3. Slowly add cheese to wine, allowing each handful to melt before adding another.
4. When cheese is fully melted, add kirsch.
5. Rub the inside of the fondue pot with the cut side of a garlic clove.
6. Transfer entire mess to the fondue pot and maintain flame hot enough to keep cheese melted but not boiling. Place fondue pot in the center of the table and let guests dive in.

swiss chocolate

1. Unwrap and serve

note Leftover cheese can be refrigerated and reheated.
specialized cooking apparatus grater; fondue pot
music to party by *The Sound of Music: Original Motion Picture Soundtrack.* The hills are alive.
recommended wine Fendant. This very dry white Swiss wine with a tiny bit of effervescence is the traditional Swiss accompaniment for fondue. Unfortunately, it is not widely accessible in North America. A Chandon Blanc or any other light, crisp white wine with high acidity will cut the richness of the cheese.

GUEST ASSIGNMENTS

1. fondue pot (to be begged, borrowed, or stolen), and candles or Sterno
2. 4 carrots; 3 heads Belgian endives; 1 red pepper and 1 head broccoli (or other seasonal vegetables)
3. 1 pound Emmental (Swiss cheese)
4. 1 pound Gruyère
5. 1 (375-ml) bottle kirsch
6. 2 loaves crusty French, Italian, or sourdough bread
7. 1 pound Toblerone, or other Swiss chocolate

Host Requirements

1/4	cup flour
1/4	teaspoon nutmeg
	salt and pepper
3	cups dry white wine
1	clove garlic
1/4	cup olive oil
2	tablespoons Dijon mustard
3	lemons
1	tablespoon honey
1	shallot
1/4	cup balsamic vinegar

POT LUCK PASTA PARTY

★ bruschetta di prosciutto ★ pasta fresca ★ romaine salad ★
★ chocolate-covered biscotti ★

a dinner for 8

Pasta (the noodle formerly known as spaghetti) is the great leveler of Italian cuisine. It's a staple in the diets of peasants and aristocracy alike. Many accompanying sauces are simmered for hours, if not the whole day. This version relies on the strong, bright flavors of its ingredients to do all the hard work. In fact, the faster it's cooked, the better it tastes—which makes it perfect for "not luck" parties.

bruschetta di prosciutto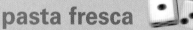

This simple version of bruschetta is another example of how a handful of common ingredients can add up to more than the sum of its parts. It's a great way to keep hungry diners at bay while dinner is cooking—and so easy to assemble that you can feel confident in assigning the task to any guest.

1	loaf rustic country-style or sourdough bread, *sliced thick*
4	cloves garlic
1/4	cup best available olive oil, or infused oil (see page 139)
1/2	teaspoon salt, or to taste (Use coarse sea salt, if you have it.)
1 1/2	teaspoons coarsely ground black pepper, or to taste
1/3	pound prosciutto (see page 135)

1 Toast the bread in a toaster or oven until it is very brown.
2 Immediately after removing the bread from the toaster, rub a garlic clove over the entire surface of one side. Each slice should use up about 1/4 to 1/3 of a clove.
3 Drizzle olive oil overtop each slice. Sprinkle with salt and a generous amount of pepper. Top with one or two slices of prosciutto. Slice into 1-inch strips, or quarters, and serve immediately.

pasta fresca

During the summer, take advantage of the juicy, flavorful tomatoes available at roadside stands.

1	cup kalamata olives, *pitted and coarsely sliced*
12	medium-size tomatoes, *diced*, or 2 (28-ounce) cans Italian roma tomatoes, *drained*
3	teaspoons salt
1/2	cup olive oil
12	cloves of garlic, *minced*
4	large shallots, or 2 small onions, *diced*
1	cup walnut pieces, or pine nuts
1	teaspoon dried chili peppers, or 1/2 teaspoon cayenne pepper
2	cups lightly packed fresh basil, *coarsely chopped*
2	teaspoons freshly ground black pepper
8	servings of fresh or dried pasta—any style or flavor
4	ounces Parmigiano-Reggiano (see page 135), *grated just before serving*

1 Assign one guest to pit the olives and another to dice the tomatoes.
2 Bring 12 cups of water and 2 teaspoons of salt to a boil in a large pot.

3 At the same time, in a large pot over medium-high heat, add $^1/4$ cup olive oil along with the garlic, shallots, and walnuts. Stir occasionally for 6 minutes, or until they begin to turn golden.
4 Add the basil, tomatoes, olives, remaining salt, pepper, chili pepper, and remaining $^1/4$ cup of olive oil. Cook for 10 minutes, stirring occasionally.
5 While sauce simmers, add pasta to the boiling water. Cook according to package directions.
6 Drain pasta, then add to sauce in pot. Toss thoroughly. Serve directly from pot or a serving bowl.
7 Serve with parmesan cheese.

romaine salad

Just a plain and simple salad. How refreshing.

2	heads romaine lettuce, *outer leaves discarded, washed and dried*
$^1/3$	cup simple vinaigrette (Make up your own, or see page 138.)

1 Toss just before serving.

chocolate-covered biscotti

1 Arrange on a plate and serve.

specialized cooking apparatus two large pots
music to party by *Tosca.* Puccini's one-hundred-year-old opera. Look for a Callas/Di Stefano version.
recommended wine Chianti. This classic Italian wine can match the acidity of the tomatoes and stand up to the strong herbs and spices in the sauce.

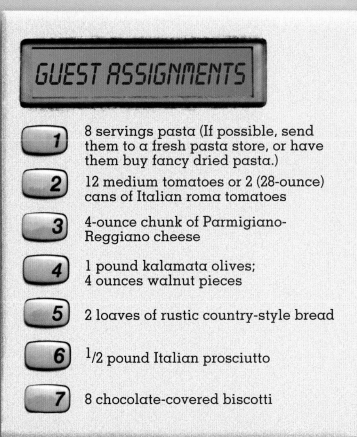

GUEST ASSIGNMENTS

1 8 servings pasta (If possible, send them to a fresh pasta store, or have them buy fancy dried pasta.)

2 12 medium tomatoes or 2 (28-ounce) cans of Italian roma tomatoes

3 4-ounce chunk of Parmigiano-Reggiano cheese

4 1 pound kalamata olives; 4 ounces walnut pieces

5 2 loaves of rustic country-style bread

6 $^1/2$ pound Italian prosciutto

7 8 chocolate-covered biscotti

Host Requirements

$^3/4$	cup olive oil
4	large shallots
1	teaspoon dried chili pepper salt and pepper
2	heads garlic
2	cups fresh basil
$^1/4$	cup vinaigrette dressing
2	heads romaine lettuce

POT LUCK PIZZA PARTY

★ **assorted olives** ★ **sliced tomato salad** ★ **presto pizza** ★ **gelato** ★

a dinner for 8

When the moon hits the sky like a big pizza pie, that's a party.

assorted olives

1 Serve as a predinner nibbly.

sliced tomato salad

Don't let a confused sous-chef put the tomatoes on the pizza. They are to be enjoyed uncooked and barely dressed.

$2^1/2$	pounds of vine-ripened tomatoes, *sliced*
$^1/2$	medium-size red onion, *diced*
2	tablespoons olive oil
$^1/2$	tablespoon balsamic vinegar
	salt and freshly ground black pepper to taste

1 Combine all ingredients in a bowl and toss gently.

presto pizza

This unconventional pizza is a curious collection of familiar ingredients that don't always find themselves side by each on a pizza crust. Sometimes you just gotta break the rules.

2	(14-inch) prepared pizza crusts (e.g., Boboli)
2	tablespoons butter
4	ears fresh corn, *cobs husked and kernels removed with a sharp knife (see page 16)* (or 3 cups frozen corn)
1	pound fresh asparagus, *bottom third discarded and remainder cut into $^1/2$-inch pieces*
1	large grilled, smoked, or BBQd chicken breast, *diced into $^1/4$-inch cubes*
1	teaspoon freshly ground black pepper
7	ounces best-quality store-bought pesto
10	ounces Brie cheese, *skin removed and sliced into long, $^1/4$-inch strips*

1 Preheat oven to 400°F.
2 Bake pizza crusts until very crispy, approximately 8 minutes.
3 While crusts are baking, melt butter in a sauté pan over medium-high heat. Sauté corn and asparagus for 5 minutes, then add chicken and pepper and sauté for 3 more minutes.

4 When crusts are crisp, remove from oven. Spread half the pesto over each crust, followed by half the pan contents. Top each pizza with half the Brie and return to oven on a cookie sheet for approximately 4 more minutes, or until Brie has fully melted.
5 Remove from oven, slice each pizza into 8 slices, and serve immediately.

gelato

1 Scoop and serve.

music to party by Various Artists. *Eh, Paisano!* Italian-American classics featuring Dean Martin, Louis Prima, and, if that's not enough, producer Billy Vera's liner-note rant on inappropriate Italian food in America.

recomended wine Washington State Merlot. Big enough to balance the Brie and pesto, and so easy to drink.

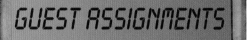

GUEST ASSIGNMENTS

1 1 pound assorted fancy olives

2 4 ears fresh corn (or 1 pound frozen); 1 pound fresh asparagus

3 1 large grilled, smoked, or BBQd chicken breast

4 2 (14-inch) prepared pizza crusts (e.g., Boboli)

5 10 ounces Brie cheese

6 7 ounces pesto (Contadina makes a very good version, available nationally in grocers' refrigerated sections.)

7 2 pints gelato (a dense Italian ice cream), or any premium ice cream

Host Requirements

2 tablespoons butter
1/2 tablespoon balsamic vinegar
2 tablespoons olive oil
salt
freshly ground pepper
1/2 red onion
2 1/2 pounds tomatoes

POT LUCK NOODLE PARTY

★ asian rice cracker mix ★ cucumber salad with fresh mint ★
★ sesame-ginger noodles with shrimp ★ freshly sliced mango ★

a dinner for 8

Despite many of the ingredients' Asian origins, no one should have to venture farther than the local grocery store for their designated ingredients.

asian rice cracker mix

1 Serve as guests arrive.

cucumber salad with fresh mint

Hand your vegetable peeler to the first person who strays into the kitchen.

3	large cucumbers, *peeled and sliced $1/8$ inch thick*
1/4	cup rice wine vinegar
1	tablespoon soy sauce
1	teaspoon toasted sesame oil
1/4	cup fresh mint, *chopped finely*

1 Combine all ingredients in a bowl and toss thoroughly.

sesame-ginger noodles with shrimp

Fresh ginger and garlic are the undertones for this rich tahini-based noodle sauce.

3/4	cup tahini (available in most grocery stores, natural foods stores, and Middle Eastern markets), *well stirred*
3	tablespoons hot chili oil (a.k.a. Mongolian fire oil)
6	tablespoons toasted sesame oil
1/2	cup soy sauce
1/4	cup rice wine vinegar
1/3	cup brown sugar (any type)
8	garlic cloves, *minced*
1/3	cup grated ginger, *peeled before grating*
8	servings of thin, Asian-style vermicelli noodles (available in most grocery stores in the Asian section), or soba noodles, or spaghetti (Yields vary, so check package.)
1/3	cup sesame seeds
1	pound uncooked, shelled, and deveined medium-size shrimp
8	scallions, *trimmed and chopped finely*
2	large carrots, *peeled and grated on the coarse side of a grater*

1 Place tahini, chili oil, 4 tablespoons sesame oil, soy sauce, rice vinegar, brown sugar, garlic, ginger, and $1 1/4$ cups of water into a blender or food processor and blend until smooth.

2 Transfer to a small pot and warm over low heat.

3 Bring 12 cups of salted water to a boil in a large pot. Cook noodles according to directions.

4 In a large, dry sauté pan, toast sesame seeds over medium heat for approximately 3 minutes. Remove and set aside in a small bowl.

5 In the same sauté pan over medium-high heat, add remaining 2 tablespoons sesame oil and cook shrimp for 1 minute per side, or until no longer translucent. Set aside in a bowl.

6 Line up 8 dinner plates. Mix the shredded carrot and scallions in a bowl and place it within easy reach, along with the bowls of shrimp and sesame seeds.

7 Drain water from noodles, then transfer noodles back to the pot. Add tahini sauce and toss thoroughly. In assembly-line style, dish the noodles onto the individual plates. Garnish with a generous sprinkle of the carrots and scallions, place several shrimp on top of each mound of noodles, and sprinkle sesame seeds overtop the whole dish. Serve immediately.

freshly sliced mango

1 Peel, pit, and slice mangoes. Fan out slices on a plate and serve.

specialized cooking apparatus blender or food processor

recommended wine Sake to me, baby. The traditional Japanese fermented rice wine is a natural pairing for many of the Asian ingredients in this dish. To heat sake, place the opened bottle in a large pot of boiling water. If you don't have a sake set, serve from a small teapot.

music to party by Cibo Matto. *Viva! La Woman.* All girls, all food. What else do you need to know?

GUEST ASSIGNMENTS

1 20 ounces dry vermicelli noodles; 8 ounces of Japanese rice cracker mix

2 10 ounces tahini

3 8-ounce bottle chili oil; 8-ounce bottle of toasted sesame oil

4 1 head garlic; 6 inches fresh gingerroot; 2 bunches scallions; 2 large carrots; 3 cucumbers; 1 bunch fresh mint

5 1 pound medium-size uncooked shrimp, shelled and deveined

6 3 ripe mangoes and/or 2 pints mango sorbet

7 8 pairs of chopsticks

Host Requirements

2/3 cup soy sauce

1/3 cup sesame seeds

1/2 cup rice wine vinegar

1/3 cup brown sugar

NOT LUCK BOUILLABAISSE PARTY

★ pâté ★ bouillabaisse ★ green salad ★ pears, grapes, and camembert ★

dinner for 8

After several trips to France, my own unsubstantiated theory about the so-called French paradox* is that it owes more to the dining habits of the French than to the red wine they consume. In France, there is virtually no takeout service and very little "fast food." Instead of eating on the fly, they take lunch and dinner *à table* with friends and linger over their meals. Without the opportunity for such idle banter, such enduring French innovations as the French kiss, the French braid, and the French fry** might never have been introduced to the world. This bouillabaisse dinner is typically served with a light red wine, which provides a perfect opportunity for you and your friends to stop and smell the rosés.

pâté

1 Thinly slice a baguette and serve alongside the pâté.

bouillabaisse

Bouillabaisse is a traditional Provençal fisherman's stew made from a vegetable-laden fish stock with a variety of fresh catches added at the last minute. Once the task of concocting the stock is behind you, the rest of this "bring your own crustacean" dinner is a snap.

advance prep for bouillabaisse stock

This stock will take about an hour to prepare and must be made before the guests arrive. It can be prepared up to 24 hours in advance and refrigerated in the pot in which it was made.

1/4	cup olive oil		6	medium tomatoes, *diced*
3	shallots, or 1 medium yellow onion, *diced*		2 1/2	cups white wine
4	cloves garlic, *minced*		2 1/2	cups clam juice
1	medium fennel bulb, "arteries" and core trimmed and discarded, chopped finely		1/2	teaspoon saffron threads
			1/2	teaspoon salt
2	stalks celery, *chopped*		1/2	teaspoon freshly ground black pepper

1 In a large pot over medium-high heat, add oil and sauté shallots and garlic for 5 minutes, or until shallots become translucent. Add fennel and celery, and stir occasionally for 10 minutes, or until all of the contents begin to show signs of browning.

2 Add tomatoes and cook for 2 more minutes. Then add wine, clam juice, saffron, salt, and pepper. Bring to a boil, then reduce heat and let simmer for 20 minutes.

3 Allow stock to cool, then refrigerate until guests arrive.

bouillabaisse (continued)

1	(1^1/2-pound) live lobster
1^1/2	pounds mussels, *debearded if necessary (just give them a quick tug) and scrubbed*
1^1/4	pounds red snapper
1^1/4	pounds scallops (The smaller, less expensive bay scallops are the way to go here.)
^{1}/3	cup Pernod, or other licorice-flavored liqueur such as sambuca or ouzo
2	tablespoons freshly squeezed lemon juice
1	cup fresh parsley, *finely chopped*

1 Bring 3 cups of water to a rolling boil in a large pot. Add lobster, cover tightly with a lid, and steam for 8 minutes per pound (approximately 12 minutes for a 1^1/2-pound lobster).

2 Bring stock to a boil in its original pot over high heat.

3 Cut snapper and scallops (if necessary) into bite-size pieces and add along with the mussels, in their shells, to the stockpot. Stir occasionally for approximately 7 minutes, or until the fish is cooked throughout.

4 Warm 2 loaves of bread in the oven (see page 137).

5 Remove stockpot from heat; add Pernod and lemon juice.

6 When lobster is fully steamed, use a large knife to chop it, in its shell, into bite-size chunks. Be forewarned, this step will be messy because trapped water will drain out of the lobster as it is cut. Add the lobster pieces to the stockpot.

7 Line up 8 soup bowls on your kitchen counter, assembly-line style. Ladle finished stew into the bowls. Discard any mussels that have not opened, and draw the colorful lobster pieces to the top of each bowl. Garnish with a sprinkle of parsley and serve immediately. Don't forget the bread in the oven.

green salad

Do as the French, and serve this salad after dinner.

3	medium-size lettuces, *washed and dried*. (Choose 3 different lettuces if available.)
^{1}/3	cup simple vinaigrette (Make up your own, or see page 138.)

1 Toss just before serving.

* In 1990, researchers discovered that the French have a very low rate of heart disease—despite their high consumption of fatty foods. The researchers hypothesized that red wine, a French staple, contains miracle-working, cholesterol-separating enzymes that counteract the fats and keep the arteries clear. The phenomenon was dubbed the "French paradox."

** Credit where credit's due department: French fries were actually invented by the Belgians.

pears, grapes, and camembert

1 Core and slice pears. Serve alongside grapes and cheese.

specialized cooking apparatus 2 large pots with lids
specialized serving apparatus 8 bowls
recommended wine Rosé from the south of France. This traditional pairing is based on regional availability and the fact that the wine is balanced enough to stand up to the garlic—but delicate enough to let the beautiful flavors of the seafood shine through.
music to party by Dimitri from Paris. *Sacrebleu*. Esquivel for the dance floor (or the dinner table, if it's sturdy).

GUEST ASSIGNMENTS

1 1 pound of pâté (or 1/2 pound each of two types); 3 loaves of crusty French bread

2 1 1/2 pounds fresh mussels*

3 1 1/4 pounds red snapper fillet*

4 1 1/4 pounds bay scallops*

5 1 1/2-pound live lobster *

6 1 (375-ml) bottle of Pernod

7 1 pound Camembert; 2 ripe pears; 1 bunch of grapes

Host Requirements

1/4   cup olive oil
1   bunch parsley
3   shallots
4   garlic cloves
1   fennel bulb
2   stalks celery
6   tomatoes
2 1/2   cups white wine (for stock)
2 1/2   cups clam juice
1/2   teaspoon saffron threads
2   lemons
        salt and pepper
        greens for a simple salad
1/4   cup vinaigrette dressing

*Empower your guests to make an executive decision if any of the seafood is not in season.

enlightening morsels

wine wisdom, kitchen counseling, and guerrilla shopping tactics

As I transformed myself from a toast-burning kitchen neophyte to a full-time foodie and professional bon vivant, I developed my own approach through trial and error. Most of this style evolved from my hedonistic quest to make a noticeable—and usually instant—impact on the quality of my cooking, dining, and drinking experiences. The following section presents a selection of my most useful discoveries and some perspective to help you steer clear of the stuff that affects your social status more than your palate.

empower yourself!

wine wisdom

I have always loved wine, but until recently I was frustrated and intimidated by the secret language and rituals of the swirling, gurgling, nosing, wine-drinking cognoscenti. Deep down, it bugged me that they seemed to know so much more than I did. Part of me was also suspicious that all the fuss was a classic case of "the emperor's new clothes." In an attempt to tutor myself, I invested in a couple of mixed cases of wine and dived in—corkscrew-first. Against my will, I was sucked in and quickly discovered that once you learn to trust your own instincts, the great mysteries unmask themselves— regardless of where you are on the wine chain. As a bonus, once you demonstrate an interest in wine, people come out of the woodwork to share their knowledge (and wine) with you.

looking for love   Wine is a very personal matter. There is no reason that you should be attracted to what everybody else likes—even if the "experts" gush about it. To empower yourself to find the wines that please *your* palate, start by paying attention to every glass you drink. Scribble notes, save labels, and steal a taste from everybody's glass the moment they turn their back. Eventually, you will notice that the wines you prefer share certain characteristics. In all likelihood, the common denominator will be the varietal (type of grape) that the wine is made from. Once you have discovered the varietal(s) you like, you have arrived at the real beginning of your wine enlightenment. From that point, you can go on to compare and determine for yourself the specific regions and producers within that genre—and within your budget—that please you the most. And don't be surprised if, over time, your tastes evolve.

one is the loneliest number   Wine, like sex, can be enjoyed alone, but is infinitely more pleasurable when paired with the right partner. Some fine wines, such as very dry Bordeaux, actually suffer when consumed without food because they need protein to counterbalance their tannins (one of the sources of their dryness). Once you have led yourself to wines you like, the next challenge is understanding the art of matching them with food. Forget the antiquated rules of food-and-wine pairing. Just think in broad strokes and let common sense guide you to wines that enhance the flavors of specific dishes. Accompany highly flavored foods with full-bodied wines that can stand up to their pungent ingredients. For example, hearty reds such as Italian Barolos, Zinfandels, or California Cabernets are all logical accompaniments for well-seasoned red meats. Medium-bodied reds like a French Burgundy or a California Pinot Noir (both made from the same grape) are most suitable for milder flavors, such as a simply prepared piece of salmon or an herb-roasted chicken. In the whites, a crisp, dry Sauvignon Blanc or French Chablis will cut through shellfish or seafoods that are naturally rich (e.g., scallops or lobster), or prepared with lots of butter, cream, or oil. California Chardonnays, often described as being "oaky" or "buttery," are able to hold their own when served with spicy dishes and can also provide a favorable foil for leaner foods, such as a simply prepared piece of fish or chicken, or simple grilled vegetables. And so on. At a more advanced level of food-and-wine pairing, wines are selected for their natural levels of acidity, sweetness, and fruitiness, to enhance or counter-balance the fats, sugars, salts, spices, and acids of the food they are paired with. There are so many guidelines that it is dizzying to try to digest them all at once (and some even seem to contradict each other). Every entrée in this book is accompanied by a wine recommendation, and the pairing charts on page 127 provide additional guidance. You can also wing it and let logic and instinct rule. Eventually, you will discover the combinations that appeal to you and gain the confidence to boldly go where no wine snob has gone before. My favorite fusion is a full-bodied Cabernet Sauvignon and rich chocolate cake.

don't swallow Different parts of your tongue are sensitive to different tastes. The tip senses sweetness; the sides, acidity; the back, bitterness; and the middle, salt. To fully appreciate the virtues of a wine, don't swallow immediately—roll it all around your tongue and savor the full range of its characteristics. (For those of you with pierced tongues, try not to dribble.)

waiting to exhale There is a lot of mystique attached to the rituals of decanting wines and letting them "breathe." It is true that older red wines do tend to blossom in flavor and complexity after they are uncorked and left to stand. But for a wine to breathe properly, it must be poured out of the bottle, because the amount of surface area at the neck doesn't expose enough of the juice to the air. At home, I pour the first two glasses while I am cooking and let them sit. This simplified version of decanting allows the wine in the glasses, as well as what remains in the bottle, time and room to "hyperventilate" to its heart's content. Even if you do nothing but pour it, a wine will "open up" as you drink your way through the bottle. Becoming conscious of the subtle changes takes you to the next level of awareness. The other reason for decanting is to filter out the sediment that may develop in older wines. If you are lucky enough to be drinking such a wine, keep it stationary for at least an hour. Then steadily pour it into a carafe or pitcher, being careful to trap the sediment in the last few drops of wine—which should be left in the bottle.

chill, baby White wines are typically served well-chilled (approximately 45°F). But too much chill can mask a wine's delicate characteristics. At professional tastings, white wines are tasted at room temperature so that the flavors—and imperfections—are accentuated. The next time you are drinking a nice glass of white wine, observe how its characteristics change as it warms up. The perfect temperature is the one that's perfect for *you*.

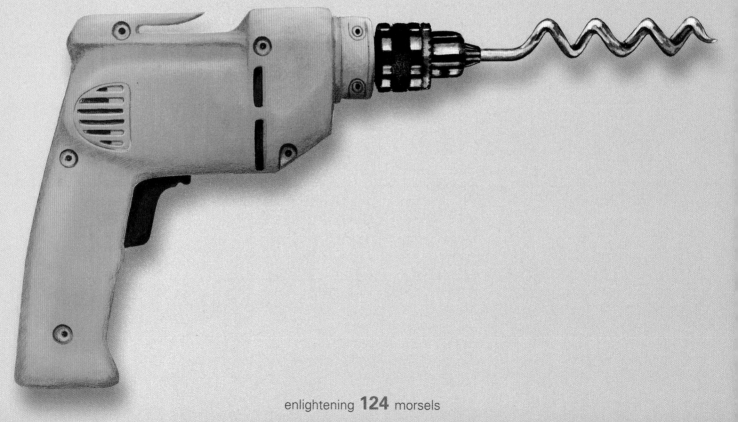

timing is everything At tastings, wines are usually served, in order, from lightest and youngest to oldest and boldest. This rule should be followed only up to the point that the taste buds remain sober. Avoid the temptation to uncork treasured bottles at the end of a night of heavy drinking—despite the inevitability that the idea will seem inspired at the time (and trust me, no one will attempt to discourage you). Save your most treasured wines for those who will appreciate them. To weed out anyone who would have preferred a Bud but didn't want to inconvenience you, use the following multiple-choice quiz: Cabernet is (A) a new Volkswagen convertible; (B) a piece of French furniture; (C) an aromatic, deeply colored grape; or (D) a trendy New York dance club.

zen is now Confucius says, "He who holds out too long for the perfect occasion, or the perfect guest, may leave behind many unopened bottles."

it never feels like the first time The company (especially a dream date), occasion, surroundings, and accompanying food can have more influence on your lingering memory of a wine than the grapes themselves. To avoid disappointment, never expect another identical bottle to ring the same bells it did the first time.

beauty is in the eye of the beholder The difference between serious wine aficionados and casual drinkers is that the aficionados take their first sip, then pause to deconstruct the nuances of the wine's bouquet, complexity, balance, "mouth feel," and "finish." Whereas casual drinkers look at the big picture and ask themselves, "Do I like this wine?" This may help to explain why someone may melt over a wine that seems uninspiring to you—and vice versa. Don't let a difference in opinion intimidate you, but do let it motivate you to give a wine a second chance. In order to ensure a fair trial under any set of circumstances, use your best efforts to block out the distractions in the room and focus your senses on what is in the glass. Sometimes the greatest distractions in judging a wine are its price, label, and reputation. A good way to block out these influences is to conduct your own blind tasting. All it takes are a few paper bags and a homemade scorecard. These tastings are fun to do with friends and inevitably produce results that are surprising, if not treasonous.

the glass menagerie Even the staunchest skeptics agree that specially shaped (read: pricey) stemware can bring you closer to a state of oneness with a wine's bouquet. It's also true that the Concorde gets you to Paris faster. Does that mean that you should take the Concorde? Only when you can comfortably afford it. Paris is still Paris. Regardless of what glass you are drinking from, make sure that it is completely free of soap and other residues. Often, glasses that look clean to the eye actually have traces of dish towel or dishwasher smell. And even perfectly clean glasses have some ambient smell. For these reasons, professional tasters pour a small splash of wine into a fresh glass, swirl it around, then dump it out before filling the glass.

wineman's bluff There is a proverb in the art world to the effect that if a work of art isn't selling, double the price. In my travels I have been privy to conversations revealing that certain winemakers inflate their prices substantially, simply as a marketing ploy. Gaga reviews and over-the-top ratings by such magazines as *Wine Spectator* can also drive the price of a wine well beyond its true market value. Abandon these "masterpieces" and search for a similar wine—with an inferior publicist. There are many other ways to stretch your wine budget. In your search for affordable, easy-drinking wines, let others do the legwork for you. A good place to discover bargain wines is at restaurants that have a designated "house" wine. Such wines are usually selected for their good value and broad appeal. If you like it, ask to see the label—and keep an eye out for it the next time you are shopping. Or stay at home and experiment. The same sixteen dollars that buys the least expensive selection on a wine list (make that twenty dollars after tax and tip) will let you feel like a big spender when you shop for wine.

just drink it Learn when to ignore everything anyone (including myself) has ever told you about wine protocol. Sometimes wine drinking, like spontaneous sex on the kitchen table, is far more satisfying when you toss out all the rules.

red wine and food-pairing wheel

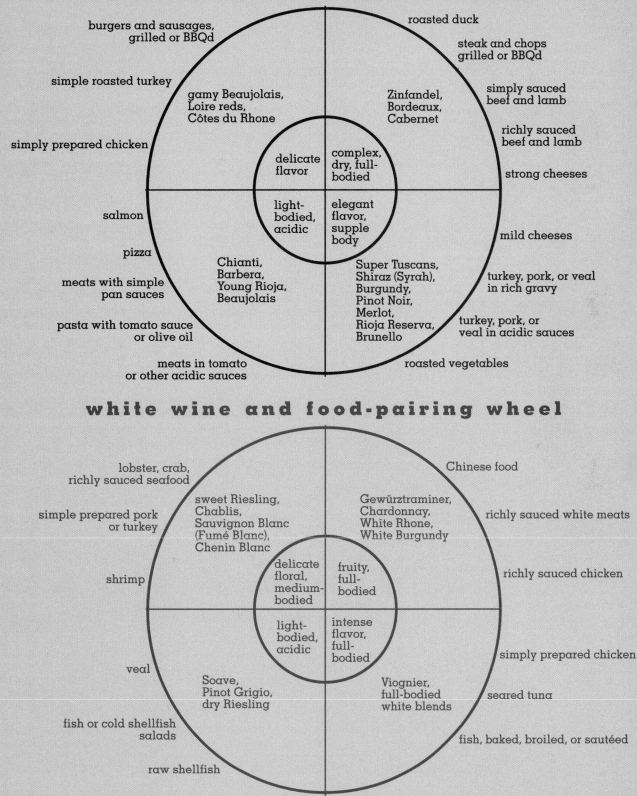

roasted duck

burgers and sausages, grilled or BBQd

steak and chops grilled or BBQd

simple roasted turkey

Zinfandel, Bordeaux, Cabernet

gamy Beaujolais, Loire reds, Côtes du Rhone

simply sauced beef and lamb

simply prepared chicken

richly sauced beef and lamb

delicate flavor

complex, dry, full-bodied

strong cheeses

light-bodied, acidic

elegant flavor, supple body

salmon

mild cheeses

pizza

Chianti, Barbera, Young Rioja, Beaujolais

Super Tuscans, Shiraz (Syrah), Burgundy, Pinot Noir, Merlot, Rioja Reserva, Brunello

meats with simple pan sauces

turkey, pork, or veal in rich gravy

pasta with tomato sauce or olive oil

turkey, pork, or veal in acidic sauces

meats in tomato or other acidic sauces

roasted vegetables

white wine and food-pairing wheel

lobster, crab, richly sauced seafood

Chinese food

simple prepared pork or turkey

sweet Riesling, Chablis, Sauvignon Blanc (Fumé Blanc), Chenin Blanc

Gewürztraminer, Chardonnay, White Rhone, White Burgundy

richly sauced white meats

shrimp

delicate floral, medium-bodied

fruity, full-bodied

richly sauced chicken

light-bodied, acidic

intense flavor, full-bodied

veal

Soave, Pinot Grigio, dry Riesling

Viognier, full-bodied white blends

simply prepared chicken

seared tuna

fish or cold shellfish salads

fish, baked, broiled, or sautéed

raw shellfish

Wine and food wheels adapted from *The Right Wine*, by Tom Maresca, with the permission of Grove Press (New York, 1990). Tom Maresca has also published a very user-friendly introduction to wine called *Mastering Wine* (Grove Press, New York, 1992).

culinary ergonomics

The following simple modifications can make even the tiniest and most dysfunctional kitchens more efficient.

designate a prep station In small kitchens, making room for adequate prep space close to the stove often requires repositioning appliances or storage jars. This reconfiguration may seem radical if the space hogs have been in the same place for ages, but as you will discover, they are not glued down. The defined area should be well lit. If you have track lighting, hop up on your counter and refocus one or more lamps to illuminate the work space (in such a way that your body won't cast a shadow where you will be chopping).

entrench the prep station Install a cutting board as a permanent fixture. If your counter surface is slippery or uneven, spread a dish towel underneath the board.

hang a dish towel within easy reach The best-ever addition to my kitchen was a two-dollar hook from the local hardware store that I screwed into my butcher block. Now, without breaking stride or looking down, I can always grab my dish towel while I am cooking (proof that one man's rags are another man's riches).

relocate your garbage bin Most kitchen garbage containers are hidden under a lid, behind the cupboard door, under the sink, several steps from the prep station. Getting to the bin with an armful of vegetable cuttings usually involves the use of multiple limbs. Like laboratory monkeys, we tend to retrace the same steps over and over without noticing the inefficiency (in fairness to the monkeys, they eventually do catch on). Conserve your energy by setting an uncovered trash bucket or bag at your feet by the prep station each time you start cooking.

essential utensils

There's a conspiracy among appliance and utensil manufacturers that is designed to eat away at our culinary confidence. The perpetrators use glossy catalogs and enticing magazine ads to brainwash us into believing it's impossible to even think about cooking unless our kitchens are fully equipped with the latest gadgetry, restaurant-style ranges, and solar-powered appliances.

Don't buy the hype. A fully loaded kitchen is not going to improve your cooking any more than the latest/greatest tennis racket will catapult you onto the lawns of Wimbledon. However, there are three basic tools that can make the game more pleasurable.

chef's knife An 8-inch chef's knife makes slicin' and dicin' a pleasure. Select one that feels solid, weighty, and well balanced in your hand. If the 8-inch blade feels too unwieldy, cradle a 6-inch model. As a general rule, if it is advertised on TV after midnight—and doubles as a saws-all—don't reach for your credit card. When in doubt, go with the name brands, such as Wüsthof, Henckels, or Messermeister. Keep your blade sharp by "edging" it regularly with a sharpening steel or a foolproof sharpener from a reliable kitchen store. If the blade gets too dull, no amount of muscle power will restore it. Bring it to a professional sharpener—it will be the most satisfying four bucks you can spend on your kitchen.

sturdy wooden cutting board A solid cutting surface—the bigger and thicker, the better—helps keep your ingredients from scattering to the four corners of your kitchen as they attempt to escape the aforementioned chef's knife.

ten-inch nonstick sauté pan and lid Life is too short to scour. SilverStone makes a fine pan for twenty-five dollars that's disposable after about a few hundred meals. All-Clad and others make pricier but virtually indestructible versions that should last a decade. Cast iron is another way to go. Once the pans are properly "seasoned " (a cooking term that describes the thin layer of oil they absorb after being coated with oil and baked for an hour at 350°F), they are as good as nonstick. Since cast iron is virtually indestructible, it makes a great flea market find.

gadgetry is the mother of convention

As further proof that cooking is about attitude, not apparatus, here are a few examples of common household objects that will help you cook just like all the other kids.

conventional item	creative alternative
martini shaker	well-cleaned teapot (note the built-in ice strainer)
ice bucket	empty 4-quart can of tomatoes with a decorative label
garlic press	chef's knife. Place the flat side of the knife on a peeled clove and pound it with your free hand. Then mince the flattened clove.
rolling pin	wine bottle
salad spinner	plastic bag whirled around your head
matching place-settings	self-confidence

shopping off the eaten path

Inspired meals are the product of inspired shopping. If you buy ingredients at the top of the flavor and freshness chain, they will heighten the flavor quotient of everything you make, give you the opportunity to create spontaneous meals, and do a lot of the hard work for you. Expand your grocery horizons and increase the diversity of your ingredients by: incorporating weekly farmers markets into your schedule; pulling over at farmers stands; patronizing local ethnic and specialty food shops; and stuffing your suitcase with local delicacies when traveling.

In conventional grocery stores, inspired shopping is one part resourcefulness and one part sheer determination. The produce person and butcher have a mandate to blow out the existing stock before replenishing the displays with the latest shipments. Leave your inhibitions behind and scrutinize for freshness by prodding and smelling. If the vegetables are limp, chances are there's a fresh crate of what you are looking for just behind the swinging doors. Sure, a surly face will meet you at the door, but once they have read your determination they will usually acquiesce. (On the surface they may seem put off by the extra work, but deep down, they will respect you for recognizing the difference.) Use these same tactics in the meat department. Remember to be appreciative. Once you make the butcher and produce person your allies, they can do lots more for you. Just for asking, they'll repackage portions, give you special cuts, and point you to the best values.

At farmers markets, many of the vendors are the actual farmers themselves—or their immediate family. When they detect even a flicker of interest in their produce, they usually become a fountain of information on everything from selection and storage to recipes.

Sometimes you have to venture beyond the familiar to get your hands on specialty items and ethnic delicacies. Turn your journey into an education by asking for samples and recommendations for products you may be unaware of. If you keep an open and inquisitive mind, the dividends for your trek will manifest themselves in the form of higher-quality ingredients and lower prices.

life support

kitchen staples I can't live without

olive oil The olive oils used in Italy are so full of flavor that often they are used in place of sauce on grilled fish and pasta. Unfortunately, many of the oils selected and marketed for American tastes are intentionally less flavorful. A good rule of thumb is that deeper-colored olive oils are more complex and flavorful, but the only way to be sure is to taste-test several varieties on small squares of bread. Some specialty food shops have sample tables so that you can try before you buy. The better oils can be much more expensive, so keep a couple of grades on hand and use the best one where its rich, nutty flavor can be easily distinguished (i.e., on delicately flavored pastas, breads, and in simple salad dressings). All oils contain the same amount of fat—even the so-called light oils. If you are trying to use less oil, use one that's more robust. A little goes a long way. Store your oil in a cool dark place.

balsamic vinegar This rich, sweet, deeply colored vinegar is aged in wooden barrels. Mass-produced balsamics start at about four dollars for a twelve-ounce bottle. Very old balsamics start at ten times that amount. I stick to the garden variety and use it to add depth to salad dressings and sauces.

salt It is easy to be skeptical about the expanding salt universe. However, salt is just like olive oil and wine. Once you tune in to the subtle differences of the good stuff, it's hard to go back. Most chefs I know cook with kosher salt in their own homes because it is free of additives and comes in a coarse form. They keep a small bowl of it beside their prep station, and when the need arises to season with salt, they pinch a bit between their fingers. The feel of the salt grains is very pleasing to the touch, and it allows more control over the amount used. For a difference you can really taste, splurge on some *sel gris* or *fleur de sel*. These are hand-harvested from sea marshes on the west coast of France. *Sel gris*, also known as *sel de Guérande*, is a coarse, grayish salt that is rich in minerals. It doesn't dissolve when it comes into contact with food, so when you bite into its crystals on bruschettas, vegetables (especially potatoes), or in salads, your mouth is filled with an intense burst of flavor. *Fleur de sel*, the very top sun-bleached layer of *sel gris*, is exponentially more expensive and even more intense. Reserve these salts for accenting foods just before serving.

whole black peppercorns Freshly ground black pepper is a must in any serious kitchen. For a coarser grind, loosen the top screw of your pepper grinder. To avoid being put through the mill yourself, buy peppercorns at bulk discount stores.

fresh herbs Fresh herbs have a totally different personality from the dried variety. Their flavors are much more immediate, especially uncooked or when added in the final stages of cooking. Many grocery stores now stock all the fresh herbs I specified in this book (cilantro, Italian parsley, rosemary, basil, oregano, thyme, mint, dill, tarragon, and sage). When cooking with these herbs, save some to add just before serving. This will "refresh" the flavor. If it is necessary to substitute dried herbs for fresh ones, a good rule of thumb is to use half the required amount. Dried herbs need heat to release their flavors, so they should be added earlier in the cooking process than fresh herbs. Crushing them in your hand before using also helps to release their flavors.

fresh garlic Accept no substitute. When buying garlic, look for a firm bulb. As it gets older and moves past its prime, the bulb loses its firmness and green sprouts appear in each clove (although not ideal, both the clove and the sprout can still be used). At all costs, avoid dried, powdered garlic, the runt of the garlic family. And be wary of elephant garlic, a much blander version of the regular-size bulb. Large garlic braids are decorative but impractical, since they often dry out before you use all of the bulbs. If you like the taste of garlic but have problems digesting it, try a trick I picked up while loitering in a restaurant kitchen in Italy: Instead of mincing the cloves, add one or two whole peeled cloves while cooking, then discard before serving. If raw garlic keeps vampires at bay, then it's a good bet that roasted garlic would make them give up their bloodsucking ways forever. Roasting garlic magically transforms each clove into a sweet caramelized jewel that bears little resemblance to the pungent bite of the raw stuff. Roasted garlic cloves are great added to pasta, salad, soup, risotto, pizza, or simply spread on a toasted baguette slice. Always make extra to keep on hand for these uses. To roast a whole bulb of garlic, slice half an inch off the pointed end of the bulb to expose each clove. Place garlic on a small sheet of aluminum foil and drizzle half a teaspoon of olive oil over the exposed cloves. Wrap and seal the foil around the bulb and bake for $1^1/4$ hours in a preheated oven at 350°F. (FYI, there is no need to buy any of those fancy-schmancy ceramic roasters; the foil works just fine.) Let it cool, then extract the individual cloves with a small fork. Refrigerate leftover cloves in the bulb, or store cloves in olive oil for up to a week. (After the roasted cloves are used up, the resulting flavored oil will have as many uses as the cloves themselves.)

shallots & leeks Both of these members of the onion family are more complex in flavor than the common off-the-rack cooking onion. When they are sautéed or baked slowly over moderate heat, their natural sugars are drawn out and caramelized. The result is a sweet, mild, almost unrecognizable version of their former selves that will add depth to sauces, sandwiches, burgers, soups, pastas, stuffings, salads, and potatoes.

lemons & limes As obvious as it may seem, these old standbys are often forgotten. Their juice and zest are worth many times their actual cost.

fresh gingerroot Fresh gingerroot adds life to many meat and vegetable dishes. Select taut, bulbous pieces. Peel and mince or grate finely when adding to marinades or soups. Use a coarser grater, or slice, for use in woks or when you want to give the taste buds (and sinuses) a real kick. Gingerroot keeps for a couple of weeks in the refrigerator and shrivels when old.

nuts Cashews and almonds are an excellent addition in stir-frys—where they can even substitute for meat. Walnuts and pine nuts (a.k.a. pignoli) can invigorate pastas, salads, and desserts. Roasting them brings out their natural richness and makes them sweeter and meatier. To roast nuts, simply spread them on a cookie sheet and stick them in an oven or toaster oven at 350°F. Bake for 5 to 10 minutes, depending on their size, until golden brown. Nuts can also be toasted in a dry skillet over medium heat for approximately the same amount of time. Nuts go rancid quickly; buy only what you can use within a month and refrigerate in an airtight container.

my pantry (on a good day) Toasted sesame oil, peanut oil, hot chili oil, safflower oil, red wine vinegar, rice wine vinegar, soy (or tamari) sauce, Worcestershire sauce, Dijon mustard, kalamata olives, canned black beans, capers, dried oregano, dried thyme, whole or ground nutmeg, ground cumin, ground cayenne pepper, fennel seeds, flour, dried pasta, rice, sugar, and honey (which I believe tastes sweeter when served from a honey bear).

current addictions

Still legal in most states.

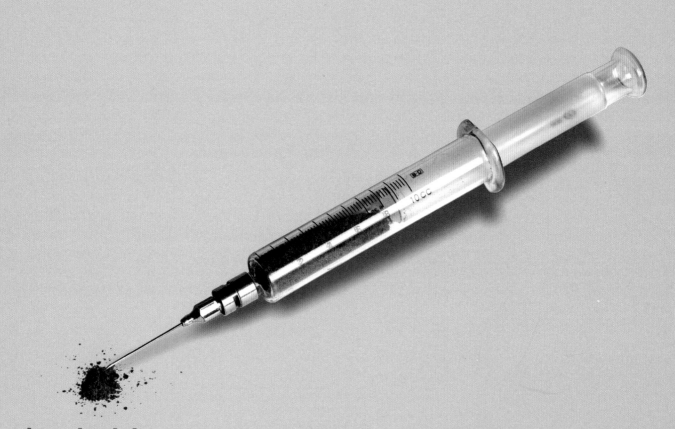

chipotle chili Chipotle chili is a Southwestern specialty made from jalapeño chilies that are smoked for days over aromatic wood cuttings. Its smoky campfire aroma imparts a distinctive spicy flavor to anything it is added to, especially salsas, chili, eggs, and dry rubs for meats. It's so addictive that I carry a vial with me to surreptitiously spice up bland meals. The dried version can be found whole or ground in specialty stores. Fortunately, it is slowly becoming available on grocery store spice racks. A canned version, pickled in adobo sauce, can also be found in Latino grocery stores.

parmigiano-reggiano Parmigiano-Reggiano is the godfather of all parmesan cheese. No other cheese tastes quite as rich and nutty as authentic Parmigiano-Reggiano, which is made from the milk of specially fed cows and aged for a minimum of two years. It is so addictive that I recently made a pilgrimage to Parma, Italy, its mecca, just to watch it being made. My curiosity was rewarded with an unforgettable lesson in Old World techniques and a three-pound wedge as a parting gift. Of the 3 million wheels produced every year, Italians consume a staggering 93 percent of them, leaving the rest of the world to fight over the remainder. It is so valuable that when Italian banks lend money to cheesemakers, they hold their 80-pound wheels of parmesan in special vaults as collateral. At about sixteen dollars a pound, it's definitely pricey, but an affordable six-ounce wedge goes a long way. (To get the most cheese for your buck, avoid pieces that have disproportionate amounts of rind.) A generous sprinkle of Parmigiano-Reggiano, grated just before serving, adds another dimension to pastas, salads, and some soups. For extra punch, use a coarser grater or wide shavings. To fully appreciate the distinctive qualities, crumble a small chunk into nugget-size pieces and nibble on them alongside a glass of hearty red wine.

prosciutto Prosciutto is the salt-cured, air-dried, hind leg of a pig. It is traditionally served in paper-thin slices. The good stuff is cured for a full year and has a unique flavor and texture that almost literally melts in your mouth. At about twenty dollars a pound, it's quite expensive—but worth every penny. True prosciutto is from the area around Parma, Italy—not coincidentally the same region where they make Parmigiano-Reggiano. The pigs are fed whey, a by-product of this rich cheese, as part of their diet. France and Spain also produce great variations, known as Jambon de Bayonne and Jamón Serrano, respectively, but they are not widely available outside of Europe. I have tasted several American versions, and I *speeet* on them all.

pancetta Pancetta is an Italian bacon that is cured with salt and spices—but not smoked. It can be found in a four-inch-diameter sausagelike roll in most Italian food shops and at many specialty butchers. Ask for slices $1/8$ inch thick. Cut it crosswise into quarter-inch strips, fry it like bacon, and add it to pastas, eggs, and salads.

maple syrup The Italians haven't totally cornered the market on my favorite regional delicacies. Maple syrup is made from the sap of maple trees, which are indigenous to Québec, Vermont, and New York State. Approximately thirty gallons of sap must be boiled down to make one gallon of syrup. As a child growing up in Montreal, I used to tap the maple tree in our front yard every spring and boil the sap in my mother's kitchen. This inevitably led to a very sticky kitchen ceiling and one measly cup of syrup. We used it on pancakes and French toast. Now, I am equally likely to include maple syrup in marinades and as a natural sugar substitute. Fortunately, the global grocery store has made it available worldwide. Grade AA is the lightest, most delicate variety, but I highly recommend grades B and C, which are darker, more flavorful, and less expensive.

portion patrol

Great food is hard to resist. However, indulging in too much of it in one sitting not only snaps you out of your culinary orgasm but sends you spiraling into a state of uncomfortable bloatedness. We've all been there. It's that I'm-never-going-to-eat-again feeling.

The prime cause of overeating is the twenty-minute delay between the time food enters the mouth and the moment the stomach signals the brain that it has arrived. That's why at a typical Thanksgiving dinner, many diners are well into their second helping of turkey, stuffing, and mashed potatoes before the stomach recognizes its predicament and sends an urgent page to the brain. Unfortunately, at this point, there's no turning back. And to make matters worse, pumpkin pie is the brain's favorite dessert.

The following tips for policing yourself and your guests are painless examples of how a little forethought can help you quit while you are ahead.

minimize the quantity of predinner nibblies
Hungry guests will usually scarf down appetizers as quickly as they are put in front of them and then look at you with puppy-dog eyes, hoping for another bone. As flattering as this may seem, don't cave. Sure it's tough love, but it does not always pay to give the people what they want.

pace the meal
Instead of serving courses one on top of the other, leave time in between, especially before dessert, for witty repartee.

serve memorable food, not memorable portions
Use garnishes and artful presentation to make less look like more on the plate.

remember, you are not being stingy with your food, you are being generous with your concern
Übereaters are always welcome to come back for seconds (after a designated waiting period).

champagne taste on a SpaghettiOs budget

Stretching your dinner party dollar.

got dough?

Artisan bakeries are popping up everywhere, and many grocery stores now make their own fresh bread. A rustic Old World loaf, an Italian or French baguette, or one of the new designer breads is a perfect accompaniment to almost any meal. Even at boutique prices, a crusty loaf is still one of the ultimate affordable luxuries.

free finishing touches

prewarm the dinner plates Method 1: Run under hot water, dry, then stack. Method 2: Stack in twos and spread around the racks of a 300°F oven for 5 minutes.

prewarm the teapot and cups Bring water to a full rolling boil. Pour about $1/2$ cup of the water into the teapot and a splash into each of the teacups. Let sit for about 30 seconds, then discard.

flavor the drinking water Add a lemon, lime, or orange slice to each water glass (okay, it's a 5¢ touch).

crisp bread or rolls in the oven Add life to bread by tossing it in a preheated 300°F oven for 5 minutes, or until it's hot and crispy. If your bread is a day old, baptize it first with a sprinkle of water.

chill the beer mugs and martini glasses Place glassware in the freezer half an hour before using.

the fifty-cent upgrade

Never let it be said that you can't afford to cook exotic-tasting food. Fifty cents' worth of fresh garlic, ginger, shallots, chilies, lime juice, or lemon zest can instantly transform any ho-hum dish into a techno-flavored rave in your mouth. By developing the confidence to add them in bold quantities, you can throw together simple meals that are as impressive as they are inexpensive.

culinary currency

Some people are lucky enough to be born with gregarious personalities that make them desirable guests. They are usually natural raconteurs or have mastered the art of making people feel good about themselves. The rest of us have to fake it . . . or make it. A kick-ass dessert, cocktail, or appetizer is great currency for the party circuit. Once you have perfected your recipe, don't hesitate to romanticize its origins or be overly protective of its "secret" ingredients. I've dined off my Caesar salad for years. If you can't come up with anything to offer, feign a love of dishwashing.

referenced recipes

roasted red bell pepper sauce

makes approximately 2 cups, enough for 2 to 4 servings

This smoky sauce will transform any plain bowl of polenta or pasta into a gourmet meal.

4	red bell peppers
1	poblano chili
2	tablespoons butter or olive oil
2	shallots, *diced*
1	leek, white and pale green section only, *diced*
1^1/2	cups chicken or vegetable stock
2	tablespoons fresh thyme, *stems removed before measuring*
2	tablespoons freshly squeezed lemon juice
	salt and freshly ground pepper to taste
^{1}/2	cup half-and-half cream

1 Roast the red and poblano peppers whole over a charcoal flame or under a broiler, turning until entirely blackened. Remove from the grill and immediately place in a paper bag, seal, and let sit for 3 minutes. Peel off the charred skin and discard. Slice open the peeled peppers and discard the membranes and seeds.
2 Melt the butter in a sauté pan over medium heat and add the shallots and leek. Cook for about 6 minutes, stirring frequently, or until the shallots and leeks are barely golden.
3 Add the stock, thyme, and half of the peppers. Bring to a boil, then immediately reduce heat to medium-low. Simmer for 15 minutes. (Adjust heat as required to maintain simmer.)
4 Remove from heat and let cool. In a food processor or blender, add the remaining red peppers, poblano chili, lemon juice, salt, and pepper. Blend until smooth.
5 Before serving, reheat sauce in a saucepan and stir in cream.

basic vinaigrette

enough to dress a salad for 4 to 6

This simple dressing will flatter any greens it is tossed with.

1	tablespoon freshly squeezed lemon juice
1	tablespoon balsamic or red wine vinegar
1	teaspoon Dijon mustard
^{1}/3	cup best-available olive oil
1	teaspoon fresh tarragon, *stems discarded before measuring*, *minced* (optional)
^{1}/2	garlic clove, *minced* (optional)
	salt and freshly ground black pepper to taste

1 Combine all the ingredients with a whisk, or in a blender or food processor.

infused olive oil

Herbed olive oils are the paramedics of the oil family. A splash will resuscitate pizzas, vegetables, and pastas, and can magically convert a plain piece of toast into a sophisticated slice of bruschetta before your very eyes.

Select a robust olive oil but don't splurge on anything too virginal—the delicate flavoring will be overwhelmed by the herbs. Stuff a selection of the following flavoring ingredients into any (well-cleaned) decorative bottle and fill with oil. As a general rule, the more ingredients the merrier. Make sure that oil covers all contents to prevent mold from forming. It generally takes about four days for flavors to impregnate the oil.

- fresh rosemary sprigs
- fresh thyme sprigs
- dried Italian herbs
- herbes de Provence
- dried chili peppers
- black or multicolored peppercorns
- peeled garlic cloves, raw or roasted (If you use these, the cloves must be removed within four days to avoid scary health problems.)

croutons

enough to top 6 servings of salad or soup

3	thick slices of slightly stale sourdough or rustic country-style bread, *cut into $3/4$-inch cubes*
3	tablespoons olive oil

1 Preheat oven to 350°F.
2 Place the bread cubes in a large bowl and add olive oil. Toss and squish the bread like a sponge until the oil is evenly absorbed.
3 Place the croutons on a baking sheet or aluminum foil and bake in the oven for 20 minutes, or until golden brown. Try not to forget about them in the oven as I often do.

simple syrup

makes 1 cup

Unlike conventional granulated sugars that have trouble dissolving in cold beverages, simple syrup blends instantly. And it ain't called simple syrup for nothin'.

1	cup water
1	cup granulated sugar

1 Boil water in a small pot. Add granulated sugar and stir until the sugar dissolves. The sweet syrup can be stored almost indefinitely in a tightly sealed jar in the refrigerator. You can adjust the yield as necessary, keeping the proportions of water to sugar equal.

basic techniques

cleaning shrimp

To devein uncooked shrimp, begin by peeling off the hard shell, then make a $1/4$-inch-deep incision with a sharp knife all the way down the middle of the shrimp's back. Use the tip of the knife to remove the thin black intestine. Some intestines will not contain any black matter. Consider yourself lucky and move on to the next one.

zesting citrus

Zest is the thin, colored, outer layer of a citrus fruit. The zest contains aromatic oils; the white part beneath it, called the pith, is bitter and, consequently, undesirable. To separate the zest from the fruit, use the fine side of a grater. If you do not have a grater, slice off the outer portion of the peel with a sharp knife, then mince it. Since you will be eating the outer peel, wash the fruit with soap and water, then rinse well and pat dry before zesting.

sealing foil packets

faux ham and eggs

smoked salmon carrots

faux diced fish

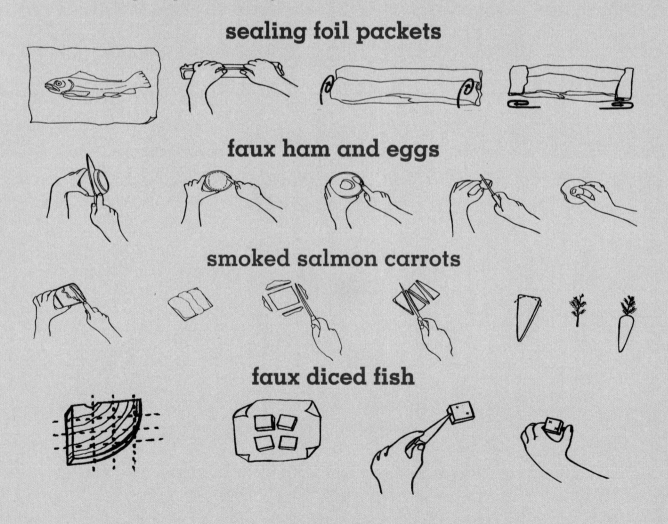

praise

To the friends, neighbors, and unsuspecting strangers who unconditionally shared their wisdom throughout the two years it took me to create this book—it's safe to answer your phone now. I am especially indebted to Aynsley Vogel for helping me craft the written word and adding a touch of class; Rodney Bowes for being as patient as he was inspired in designing the book with me; Dick Kaiser for his meticulous photography and his Zen-like wisdom; and Susan Rose for enduring my single-minded focus.

sous chefs (overworked and underpaid—but well-fed)

personal editor Aynsley Vogel; **tackle** Norman Perry; **arbiter of good (and bad) taste** Susan Rose; **sourcerer** Susi Varin; **recipe tester** Kate Sage; **agent** John Boswell

the kitchen cabinet

Alan Sasoon, Alex Klapwald, Allison Wright, All-Clad, Alison Emilio, Amy Alkon, Andy Zimbel, Ange Stevenson & John Ludgate, Angela Freire, Bev Chin, Bob Aschmannn, Bob Donalson ("Winner Dinner" lettering), Brian Barrington, Carrie Pillar, Cathy Cleghorn, Charisse Glenn, Chris DeVita, Cinderella Dietrich, Claire Coates, Claire Contamine, Clarissa Troop, Catherine Thelia, Colleen Woodcock, Daniella Dornicak, David Sanfield, David Talbot, Debbie & Aisha Jow, Diana Riesman & Fred Cowett, Doug Mark, Edgar, Teddy & Alistair Moss, Eleanor Mondale, Emily Grayson, Emma Pearson, Erika Geiger, Erin Smith, Evie Truxaw—Tierra Vegetables, Fred Eric, "Gaucho" Jack Blumer, Heidi Diamond, Heidi Von Palleske, Jacki Fitzgibbon, Jami Galbraith, Jamie Price, Jane Siberry, Jeff Smith, Jenn Shreeve, Carol Boswell, John & Margie Loken, Jon & Dede, Judith Curr, Karolina, William, Louis and Narine—Rush Copy, Kate Rivington, Kevin Laffey, Laurie Kahn, Lesley, Button & Marty Hollenberg, Lori Tieszen, Marc & Amy, Marilyn Pocius, Margaret Johnstone, Margo McNeely, Marla Ceresne, Mary Ann Gilderbloom, Mary Burnham, Mary Duff & Peter Ortale, Mary Sue Milliken, Mayfair Market—Franklin, Maureen & Pat Doherty, Matt Zimbel, Ml Compton, Michelle Bega, Mimi, Monica Netupsky, Mrs. Dash, Mus—The Red Bench, Nancy Silverton, Nion McEvoy, Patrice Bilawka, Patty Brown, Peter Borland, Pompea & Walter Smith—Hollywood Farmers' Market, Raymond Coffer, Rhonda Troutman, Rick Arnstein, Robert Phillips, Romily, Soph & Rylan Perry, Sandra Dewey, Sandy Castonguay, Sasha Galbraith, Sarah, Blair, Olivia & Charlotte Damson, Skip King, Stephanie Kelmar, Stephen Grynberg, Steve Perrine, Steve Waxman, Tracey Reid, Marian Temesvary & Elizabeth Karmel—Weber, T. J. Nelson, Walnut Pesto & Cherry Pie.

wine gurus (hard work if you can get it)

Andrea Immer, Christian Navarro, Darryl Roberts, Joel Quigly, Kelly Bernard, Stewart Dorman, Steve Wallace, Terry Robards, Tom Maresca.

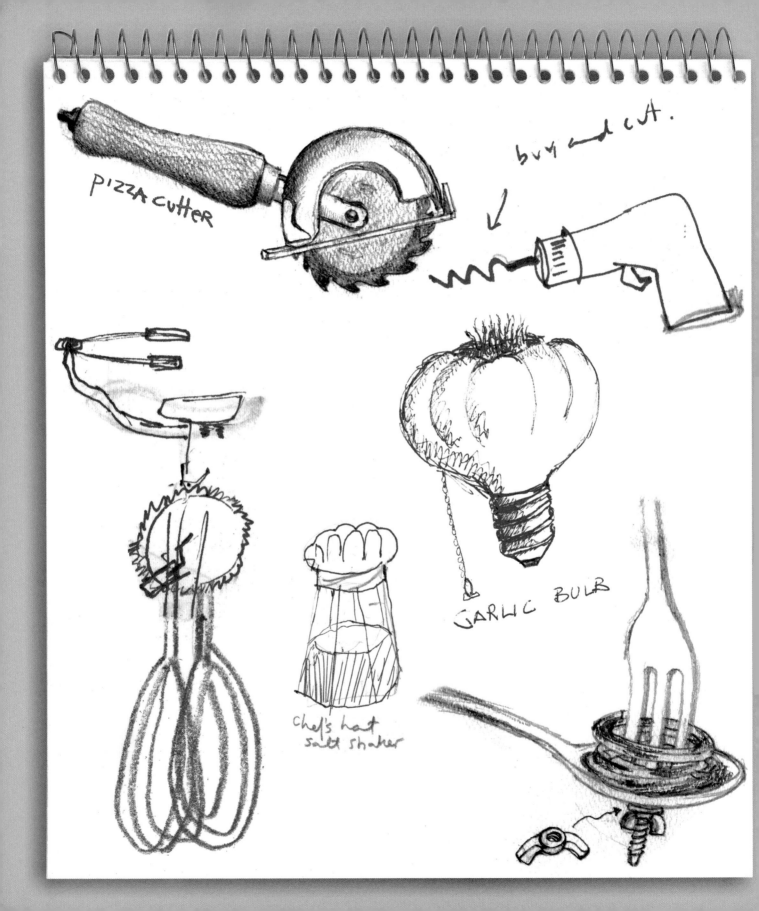

about the art

art direction "analog Bob" Blumer & "digital Rodney" Bowes.

illustrations Bob Blumer. All Illustrations were hand-rendered in acrylic paint on Strathmore cold-pressed illustration board.

wine and martini glasses Bob Blumer. The original versions of these glasses were commissioned by the Salvador Dali Museum in Saint Petersburg, Florida, for a fund-raising event. They are made from standard-issue restaurant glassware, cut with a ceramic tile "rod saw," then glued to their base with five-minute epoxy.

bric-a-brac The guerrilla grilling mitt and paper bag chef's hat were stitched by Susan Rose (scrose@flash.net). All other objets d'art were fabricated by Bob Blumer from mixed media and found objects.

photography Dick Kaiser (dbkaiser10@aol.com) is a Los Angeles–based photographer. His experience as an ad agency art director and his keen eye for detail have made an invaluable contribution to all three Surreal Gourmet books.

food styling No food was harmed or manipulated for the food photography. All meals and cocktails were made by the author exactly according to the recipes and photographed (and subsequently devoured). What you see is what you'll eat.

design and computer graphics Rodney Bowes (rodney.bowes@sympatico.ca) is a globally based graphic designer. He has won numerous awards for projects ranging from album package design, to corporate brochures, to soda pop labels.

cover image The cover concept was executed in Vienna, Austria, by digital wunderkind Andreas Fitzner, co-owner of Vienna Paint (vip@viennapaint.com). Cover photography by Dieter Brasch.

For kitsch 'en stuff, including books, original illustrations, limited-edition prints, one-of-a-kind glassware, aprons, other assorted fruits of surreal inspiration and garlic-induced hallucinations:

call 1 800-FAUX-PAS
surf http://surrealgourmet.com
e-mail mall@surrealgourmet.com
post The Surreal Gourmet, P. O. Box 2961, Hollywood, CA 90078 USA

The Surreal Gourmet

The Surreal Gourmet Entertains

books

Adventures in Entertaining
signed lithograph 21" x 30"

Hollywood Farmers Market
poster 18" x 24"

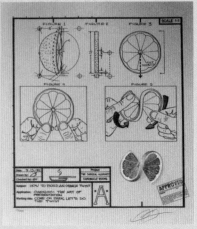

Orange Twist Blueprint
signed silkscreen/collage 18" x 21"

posters

the **144** end